SINNED AGAINST

EXPLORING THE SCRIPTURES

VALERIE WRESSELL

IM¶RESSUM

First published in 2020 by Impressum
50 Wimbledon Grove, Garden Suburb NSW 2289 Australia
www.impressum.com.au

10 9 8 7 6 5 4 3 2 1

Copyright © Valerie Wressell 2020

All rights reserved. No part of this book may be reproduced or transmitted in any form or by any means, electronic or mechanical, including photocopying, recording or by any other information storage retrieval system, without prior permission in writing from the publisher.

All Scripture quotations, unless otherwise indicated, are taken from the Holy Bible, New Revised Standard Version® Anglicised NRSV®. Copyright ©1989. Used by permission. All rights reserved worldwide.

Scripture quotations marked 'NLT' are from the New Living Translation, copyright ©1996 by Tyndale House Publishers Inc. the Wheaton, Illinois. Used by permission. All rights reserved worldwide.

ISBN: 978-0-6487074-4-8 (paperback)
ISBN: 978-0-6487074-5-5 (ebook)

 A catalogue record for this book is available from the National Library of Australia

Cover photography by Eve Wressell
Design by Brugel Creative

For Jenny, Eve and Daniel and their families, with all my love.

This verse has guided my steps from the
beginning of my Christian journey–

Nehemiah 4:14 …Remember the LORD, who is great and awesome, and fight for your kin, your sons, and your daughters…

COMMENDATIONS

❝This work opens our minds to the great love God has for us, an honest reminder that God is with us no matter what, and how He shapes our lives for His glory, even out of being *Sinned Against*. This book will be used as the backbone in the spiritual development of those recovering from DFV in the Peninsula Lighthouse program.❞

~ Natasha McDowell, CEO Peninsula Lighthouse, Australia

❝Inspirational books are ones that describe tough personal experiences, bringing stories of triumph out of deep and wounding adversity and abuse. This is one such book. In *Sinned Against* Valerie Wressell has drawn on real life personal events to guide the reader in exploring recovery and healing, as she sensitively applies Bible promises, and reveals a God engaged and available during life's toughest seasons. As an individual read or in a group context, your investment reading *Sinned Against* will leave you informed, inspired and reassured that you are never alone.❞

~ Rev. Andrew Dawkins, Pastor Kariong Community Baptist Church, Australia

MY THANKS

This book would simply not have come about without the contributions of very many people not only toward the content and the publishing of the book, but also into my own life.

My thanks therefore go to the many people, mostly women, who worked with me during the writing and shaping of the studies. Whether in groups, or singly; whether in formal setting, or random one-off conversations in which personal stories were unexpectedly shared; all have contributed to the final outcome.

My thanks also go to the pastor who asked me if I could try and 'blokify' the content, so that it might be rendered more relevant to men who have also suffered abuse. This changed my approach to the whole project, causing me to review my writing, consider my female bias, and attempt to adapt my thinking accordingly.

My thanks go to my Bible teachers. Not only those who have taught me through Bible studies throughout the years, but more specifically to those at Morling College who taught me how to go about mining the unfathomable riches of God's word. A joy that persists.

My thanks go to fellow Christians, who, to their own cost have employed their God-given gifts, and their compassion, skill, courage and faith in God's promises to minister holistic healing to me. I simply cannot thank them enough. Without their help, I would not have gained freedom from the legacy of the abuse that I endured.

My thanks go to Sheree Chambers and Erin Sessions who have believed in my endeavours, and have facilitated the publishing of this work. It would not have been printed, or certainly not to this standard, otherwise.

My thanks, of course, go to my husband Charles, my family and my friends who have believed in the project and have supported and encouraged me to keep going.

Above and beyond all, my thanks go to the risen, living Lord Jesus Christ. He loves me, and he rescued me. He won, to his own great cost, my freedom from the fear of death, the entanglements of the world, and the legal rights of the devil. Astonishingly, he endowed me with a measure of his own Holy Spirit when I came to put my trust in him. No amount of earthly counselling could achieve what my heavenly Counsellor has done, and will continue to do in my life.

All that Jesus has done is recorded in the Bible—his own self recorded in written words—the Word of God, the Bible. What he has done for me he has done for everyone. And why he has done it is there for everyone to read for themselves. An enduring, unchanging reference to truth, living and active, on which we can depend.

It is my prayer that through this book, God will connect people with his living Word, and by his Holy Spirit multiply to others the blessings I have received. Thank you, Jesus.

Valerie Wressell

CONTENTS

Commendations v

My thanks vi

Foreword xiii

Introduction 1

Section One: About God 17

    Study 1: God's grief 19
                                      Questions   28

    Study 2: Being God 34
                                      Questions   44

    Study 3: God's sovereignty 48
                                      Questions   59

    Study 4: God with us 63
                                      Questions   71

    Study 5: Mission accomplished? 76
                                      Questions   87

Section Two: About Ourselves 93

Study 6: What's in a name? 95
Questions 103

Study 7: Sticks and stones 107
Questions 117

Study 8: Shame on you! 122
Questions 132

Study 9: Who's to blame? 136
Questions 146

Study 10: Silence is golden? 151
Questions 160

Section Three: About How We Relate to Others 165

Study 11: Where the rubber hits the road 167
Questions 176

Study 12 Mind how you go 180
Questions 191

Study 13: A profound mystery 195
Questions 206

Study 14: Forgive them Father 211
Questions 220

Study 15: Sure of what we hope for............224
                                            Questions 234

Appendices.................................239

    Appendix 1: The Garden of Gethsemane:
    A reflection.............................241

    Appendix 2: A brief word for group leaders........249

Bibliography...............................255

About the Author 259

FOREWORD

If you have picked up this book because of the title, it is quite possibly because it has resonated with your own experience, or with that of a close family member or friend of yours who has been significantly sinned against. However, everyone will have experienced some form of injury, whether physical, mental, material, financial, emotional or spiritual, as the result of someone else deliberately causing them harm. From having a crayon stolen from you in kindy, to experiencing the worst of atrocities too awful to be shown on the evening news, no one escapes. So much so that we can take it for granted that this sort of behaviour is a part of everyday life, against which we have to be on guard.

However, because it is so common, we may hardly consider its effect on individuals and on the community in which we live. We may not even think to ask: 'Is this how God planned life on earth to be?'

As a result of this abuse, people may carry injuries, whether visible or invisible, throughout their entire lives. These injuries, left untreated, may shape the way our lives unfold, because, after all, we do not want to be hurt again. But thankfully, our situation is not without hope. Healing and restoration to wholeness are possible, and the aim of this series of studies is to communicate that hope to people who are carrying the burden of being sinned against.

I myself suffered profound abuse throughout my entire childhood, but I have also been very blessed. Blessed not only with increasing freedom and healing in Christ, but also with training and experience as a senior school teacher, a Bible study leader and the later opportunity to study not only the Bible in greater depth but also many aspects of Church ministry.

My experience and my pastoral training prompted much reflection. In researching this topic, I was shocked to discover the appalling statistics concerning the prevalence of serious abuse, of all forms, within our own society. I found I was not an oddity, or a rarity, but one of millions who have suffered at the hands of other, more powerful people. It therefore seemed a logical progression that my heartfelt desire to share the blessings I have received with others, should find distillation in this series of studies.

In order to achieve this end, I have worked principally with women from two different church fellowships, as well as with individuals. Some of these women had suffered abuse, and some had not, or were not aware of having done so. Men also suffer great abuse. However, as biblical truths do not change on account of gender, or age or race or social status, hopefully any seeming gender bias will not be a hindrance to men also benefitting from these studies.

In addition to childhood abuse, the women in the original project group had suffered domestic violence (which is far more than just physical violence), and planned and random sexual assault, including gang rape. We brainstormed all the issues that we could think of that give rise to difficult questions concerning God. These included such issues as justice, rage, forgiveness, self-esteem, guilt, secrecy, security, trust and so on. We then grouped related topics together for the purposes of writing the Bible study. As we progressed, a 'shape' for the series emerged.

Firstly, it seemed we needed to sort out our thoughts about God, concerning his character and his purposes for his creation. These included the challenging problem of a supposedly good and all-powerful God allowing or possibly even orchestrating really bad events in our lives.

Having explored 'Right thoughts about God', we then progressed to tackling the topics concerning right thoughts about ourselves. Topics such as shame and blame, self-worth and identity. Finally, we found we could tackle topics related to right attitudes toward other people, which of course included forgiveness, and love and 'What does victory even look like?'

However, this order of tackling these studies is only a suggestion. I have also worked through these studies backwards with some women who really wanted to jump in at the 'forgiveness' part of the series. God will meet us at our point of greatest need, wherever that is.

WHY A BIBLE STUDY?

Since starting this venture, I have spoken with any number of people about the project only to discover that often, the conversation seems to give permission for them to share situations of abuse they have suffered, of which I knew nothing, and that they have never spoken about before in a Christian context.

I have discovered that it is more difficult to find someone in an ordinary Church, particularly among the women, who has not suffered some form of significant abuse in their life, than someone who has. Looking on from the outside people seem to be coping just fine. Most have perhaps escaped their abusive situations and are just getting on with life, putting what happened behind them as best they can. Jesus has gathered them into his church, but the wounds remain, tucked away, unseen and unhealed. There are simply not enough qualified counsellors to help all these people.

Neither am I a qualified counsellor or psychologist. I do not know, and have not heard, the griefs of hundreds or thousands of different people as they seek to be free of the effects of past abuse. In fact, I find it hard to even read the sufferings of other people. However, to God, nothing is tucked away unseen, and his heart is to bring the oppressed, the heartbroken, and those held in captivity into freedom and victory in Christ (Lk 4:18–19). And to this end he has provided not only his son Jesus, but also his Word and his Spirit.

The Word of God is unique within the whole global library of writings because it is God's words, spoken out and written down by people. Like God himself, it is living and active and can reach right into the innermost parts of our beings to bring illumination, conviction, instruction, teaching, healing, and restoration—indeed anything that is ultimately for our good. Human wisdom unconnected with spiritual counsel can accomplish much, but it is limited within the earthly realm of knowledge and devoid of spiritual power.

Jesus told his disciples at the last supper that he would send them a counsellor, the Spirit of truth, the Holy Spirit, who would guide them in all truth (Jn 16:13). He told them that the Spirit would teach them and remind them of everything he had said. And that, unless he went away, the Holy Spirit could not be sent. However, this same Spirit, according to Paul is also the Spirit of Christ (Ph 1:19). And Christ is also the Word of God (Jn 1:1–5), in effect, Jesus, written in words for us to read.

And this same Word is also the sword of the Spirit—"...living and active, sharper than any double-edged sword, piercing until it divides soul from spirit, joints from marrow; it is able to judge the thoughts and intentions of the heart" (Heb 4:12).

Thus Jesus, Word and Spirit are all of God and all work powerfully together to accomplish the will of God—victory in Christ, in people's lives. This is why I have written these studies—in the hope of connecting people with the truth about their situations in Scripture with a view to pursuing healing.

Some survivors of abuse will very much need the help of doctors, skilled counsellors and psychotherapists in their journeys to victory. I myself am one of these. However, I also know, from my own experience, and the work I have so far done with this series of studies, that God can and does do astonishing things as people open themselves to, and embrace, the truth that is written in his Word and empowered by his Spirit.

INTRODUCTION

ABOUT ME

I didn't think anything of it at first. Why should I? All I knew was that the truth I had been diligently pursuing, concerning God, was now made wonderfully and simply plain to me. Although I saw nothing with my eyes, I knew without a shadow of a doubt that the One who keeps the earth spinning on its axis was visiting with me in my living room! I was aware of an indefinable power which somehow communicated to me that I was utterly and perfectly loved, and that this love would endure throughout eternity.

This was a bit confronting for me who, until that moment, hadn't consciously believed in the reality of the world of spirit, nor life into eternity. Nor had I realised that the one thing my heart had been yearning for all my life was this perfect, never-to-be-broken love relationship. I say 'relationship' because what could I do but love in return? My life at that moment was turned on *its* axis, reorienting itself entirely so as to follow Jesus, just as a compass point will turn to face north.

It wasn't until later that I came to realise that apparently many people, on choosing to follow Jesus have recognised in themselves a need to have their sins forgiven. 'What is sin?' I asked my friend. Jesus hadn't said anything about sin to me when I chose to follow him. Why not?

She had given me a modern translation of the Bible and with this in hand, she sent me off to read the letter Paul wrote to the Christian believers in Rome. I came to understand about sin, and did indeed ask Jesus to forgive me mine, but the question remained at the back of my mind—'Why hadn't Jesus said anything to me about my sins before I started following him?'

One thing I did know was that the Bible, God's written Word to the world, was like a living thing. Truth would jump out at me from the pages, feeding my desperate hunger to know absolutely everything all at once! I would fall asleep on the sofa with the open book on my chest while my children played at my feet. The words brought knowledge, understanding, comfort and healing to me. My heart, which was rather like a dirty dried kitchen sponge, became gently plumped up and cleaned as it was soaked in the love of God.

Little did I know at the time, how much healing and cleaning were needed. My love of God's Word kept me in Bible study groups throughout the years, but once the children were grown up, I took the opportunity to study God's Word more intensively full time, at Bible College. It was at this time that God chose to do more challenging work within me as he began to bring healing for physical, mental, spiritual and emotional hurts sustained during the profound abuse I experienced throughout my entire childhood. And this is when my question began to be answered.

I came to understand that Jesus meets us where our need is greatest. It is surely true he came to pay the debt we owe to God because of our rebellion against him—we are all included in that blessing if we choose to accept it. But he also came to minister healing and justice to the sinned against. All throughout Scripture God reminds his people again and again to care for the powerless, which include the widows and the orphans, the poor, the blind, the hungry, those who are oppressed, enslaved or in prison, and the landless who had no means of providing for themselves (Deut 24:14–22; Ps 72:12–14; Mal 3:5).

Jesus announced his ministry to these 'sinned against' people in the synagogue in Nazareth (Lk 4:16–19). He was reading from the book of Isaiah, which prophesied that the wounds of the broken hearted would be bound up, those held captive would be set free, those who mourned would be comforted and all debts would be cancelled. Grief would be translated into joy and praise, the weak and faint would become strong, like oak trees planted by the LORD. "For I the LORD love justice, I hate robbery and wrongdoing" (Is 61:1–3).

On checking out Jesus' ministry in the gospels, I noted that when he is among the people, he sometimes, but not always, pronounced forgiveness of sins. Sometimes he provided physical healing, and sometimes deliverance from spiritual oppression. Sometimes he would give a challenging word, and sometimes a word of comfort. If needed, he would restore the person to their community, a place of belonging and acceptance. On occasion he restored life itself, where there had been death. He met people where they were, and according to their primary need at that time.

I understand now that Jesus knew my first need was not to know that my sins were forgiven. I had, after all, tried to do everything perfectly, as there had been times when my very life depended on it. He knew that my first need was to know that I was utterly loved, no strings attached, and that I would never be betrayed by this One who loved me, ever. So what was my response?

One of Jesus' disciples wrote: "We love because he first loved us" (1 Jn 4:19). This is what happened to me. I could hardly help loving Jesus in response to his love for me. And to love Jesus meant that I would choose to orientate my life to follow him. Other, more detailed explanations would come later as and when God knew I could cope with them.

Indeed, more detailed explanations are very necessary. Abuse prompts many difficult questions concerning the character of God, the value of a human soul, and the appropriate response of a survivor to the injuries which were sustained. These deserve thoughtful answers. In this book, my aim has been to guide the reader to consider their own answers to these questions as they engage with the Word of God, the Bible. It is here that we find truth, about God and about ourselves and our world. It is this truth that will set us free to embrace life in all its fullness.

It is my hope and prayer that through engaging with God's Word in this study, many of you who are among the sinned against will be helped to discover God's true character, and your true worth, and be enabled to move forward in life in the victory Jesus has so fulsomely won for you.

WHAT ABOUT YOU?

Where are you from, what is your background and what is your story?

This study is firmly based in the Holy Bible, a collection of 66 books written by many different people over a period of thousands of years. Some of these books, now grouped into the Old Testament were written before Jesus lived on earth, and some of them, which make up the New Testament, were written after Jesus' time. They contain the true stories of actual people who lived and walked on this earth. Perhaps you are familiar with the stories, perhaps not.

How do you understand this world you live in and how you fit into it? Have you ever heard of Jesus or been told his story? Perhaps you come from a culture that is not based on Christian principles but on those of another religion. Maybe you have never had the opportunity to find out who this man Jesus was and why he suffered so terribly and died. If so, it may help to read this brief account of the biblical worldview, and how Christians seek to work out how they are to live their lives in light of their understanding of God.

Christian worldview

Christians believe that we have only one life, here on earth. We also believe that each human spirit endures into eternity, and that it does not become absorbed into a larger 'life force'. That is, we will always be who we are. However, once our body dies, the destination of our eternal spirits—whether in heaven, or in hell—depends on the choices we make concerning God, here and now, while we have breath.

We read in the Bible that there is but one living God who, puzzlingly, manifests in three Persons—Father, Son (Jesus Christ) and Holy Spirit. This is hinted at even on the first page of the Bible, as God said, "Let us make people in our image, to be like ourselves." And so it was that God created humankind and the universe we live in by his spoken Word, and it was "very good"—in the beginning.

We also find that God loves us and longs for relationship

with us, for in his wisdom he endowed humanity alone of all creation with the gift of free will to choose to respond by loving him in return. No other living creature was granted the ability to say 'Yes' or 'No' to their creator God.

Unfortunately, the first people he created, Adam and Eve, decided they would say 'No' to God and do their own thing, contrary to God's specific instruction. This is called sin, which is rebellion against God. And because of this choice that they made, sin has affected all generations since. It also caused catastrophe throughout God's whole creation.

We also read that there is an adversary to God, who is spirit and who hates God and those who were made in God's image. This is Satan, who was instrumental in causing this rift between God and humankind. He is dedicated to doing all in his power to cause as much pain to God, and death and destruction to people as possible.

Because connection between humankind and the living God—the source of life—was severed by sin, we all inevitably die. But sin grew and flourished and within the first few chapters of the Bible we learn that the growing population of this pristine planet quickly descended into violence to such an extent that it broke God's heart.

The rest of the Bible tells us the story of how God went to incredible lengths to make it possible for all those who choose to respond to his love, to be reconnected into relationship with him, the living God. And so, to gain life eternal, even though our bodies will still eventually die.

This was finally brought about by the life, suffering, death and resurrection of Jesus Christ, God's son. This was a mission Jesus voluntarily undertook, on our behalf. All who believed he was who he said he was, and who chose to say 'Yes' to God would be considered children of God.

If you have suffered significant abuse you will have experienced the reality of sin in all its ugliness and pain. You will know that fear of death is a reality in this world. This part of the story will 'ring true' to you. As you explore the Scriptures for yourselves, may you discover, to your joy, that all the rest of the story is true too.

A WORD TO THE WELL-VERSED CHRISTIAN

Or new glasses for reading the text

If you have been studying Scripture for a long time, you may have formed fairly fixed opinions as to what a particular text might mean, or what it means to you. In this series of studies, it may be that you will find yourself looking at a text from a different point of view. It will be helpful to at least be open to alternative interpretations of familiar passages.

Our viewpoints differ

Studying the Bible by ourselves is a blessed occupation. Each of us is promised heavenly help through the Holy Spirit, who will help us to understand what it means, and who will apply it to our circumstances. However, studying in a group is great too, because we hear different answers to the study questions and get a glimpse of what the Scriptures might be saying to someone else travelling a different life journey.

Max Lucado, in his book *The Applause of Heaven*, makes reference to Jesus' teaching in the Sermon on the Mount,

"Blessed are those who mourn, for they will be comforted" (Mt 5:4).[1] I was surprised to discover that in it, he assumes that our mourning concerns the grief we may feel concerning our own sinning. And it therefore follows that this grief—feeling sorry for our sins—opens up the way to being comforted when we look to Jesus Christ to make things right between us and God.

However, when I shared this verse with the project group of ladies, every single one of them understood the verse to mean that they would receive comfort from God on account of all that they had suffered at the hands of others. In other words, the comfort they receive would be for the grief they had experienced for having been sinned against.

One verse, with two contrasting interpretations. How can this be? Is one right and the other wrong? Not at all. It is simply that the verse is being understood and applied within differing circumstances. It demonstrates that we all read Scripture through different glasses, and that it is possible to have a different understanding of a text than that which is given by someone whose circumstances are quite different.

Two different lenses to these glasses

One lens through which we read Scripture must always be the love of God. Everything we read should be understood in light of the fact that God loves each one of us and has gone to extraordinary lengths to make it possible to re-establish relationship with us. This impacts every interpretation we might make of any text. We need to remind ourselves of the crucifixion of Christ every time we read shocking, puzzling events in the Old Testament.

---

1   Max Lucado, The Applause of Heaven, chapter 5.

However, in this series of studies, the other lens through which we consider Scripture may mean that we see things that others might miss because my chief focus has been to look for the power differential in the situation. Who has the most power? Who is the powerless? This is because every abusive event arises because an offender chooses to exercise their greater power in a harmful way over their victim.

Bathsheba

For example, it may be that some would say Bathsheba was tempting King David by bathing on the roof of her house in full view of the palace, and she got what she was after; a tryst with the king (2 Sam 11). However, a careful reading of the text yields not one single reference to any sin by Bathsheba. Bathing on the roof was the way things were done in those days. The question to ask was, what was King David doing twiddling his thumbs in the palace when his armies were out fighting battles for him? The king had all power at his command. Bathsheba, a female subject, had no intrinsic power to deny him. She lost her home, her husband, and the child that was born to her. Later, however, she had a son, Solomon who succeeded David as king. What does this tell us about God, and his heart for Bathsheba?

The woman at the well

In the New Testament, Jesus spends quality one-on-one time talking to a woman at a well, one dusty hot midday (Jn 4). Many commentators refer to her as a sinful immoral woman. The effect of this is evident in the general church as person after person says to me, 'I have always thought of her as a sinful woman.' However, a careful reading of the text reveals that she was married, five times, although the man she was currently with was not a husband. What is immoral about being married?

Her context is not that of a Hollywood movie star who is marrying and discarding husbands one after the other. She is a Middle Eastern peasant woman, with no power. Women were counted as commodities who cooked and cleaned, who warmed their husbands' beds, and bore their children. She would have been passed from man to man to man to man to man as a wife, and it is not beyond the bounds of possibility that the sixth man declined to make the relationship legal. Understanding this scenario, we should ask 'What did it mean to this woman to be passed around in such a way?' 'What was the impact on her self-worth and her standing in the community?' We see that Jesus took the time to reach out to her, and restore her dignity and place in society. Indeed, she was the first believer of a fledgling Samaritan church.

Rahab

Rahab was a prostitute who features in the genealogy of Christ (Josh 2). She was rescued from Jericho with her family, and became the mother of Boaz, who married Ruth. Their son Obed was the grandfather of King David. How do we read her situation? Was God just being especially gracious in saving an immoral woman and including her in Jesus' family tree? Female prostitutes, wherever they appear in Scripture, are usually judged and condemned as immoral by readers. I have to ask, what do we think of the immorality of all the many more men who use prostitutes, who seem to slip under the morality radar?

Did Rahab choose her occupation? Can she be judged as having made an immoral choice? What little girl in primary school puts up her hand and says: 'I want to be a prostitute when I grow up.' The vast majority of such women—and men—who are prostitutes were abused as children, and have minimal or no family support. Some will have been entrapped and enslaved and made addicted to drugs. However, God does not miss a thing. He knows all of this. Jesus reached out to such people in gentleness and love. These stories should inform our reading of God's character, and his heart for the enslaved, and oppressed and powerless.

A wife

However, it is not only in the epic dramas of ancient times that we wrestle with understanding God's character. It also comes close to home, indeed right into the home, within a marriage. In a marriage in which one or both partners attend church, how often have the verses "Wives submit to your husbands as you do to the Lord. For the husband is the head of the wife just as Christ is the head of the church…" been used in an attempt to control a wife's behaviour (Eph 5:22-23)? What was God thinking in including this text in the New Testament? We will explore this topic in detail in Study 13 *A Profound Mystery*. But what do we see by carefully reading the whole text while looking at it through the lenses of a loving God and a power differential (Eph 5:21-33)?

The actual outworking of this intimate relationship before God is subject to much debate. Opinions on this matter differ, because man and woman are created equal in value, dignity and purpose before God, and before each other. (See Study 12, *Mind how you go* 'Concerning man and woman'). Woman was not made to be subservient to man, but to be a co-worker of equal status. Both are to work together in ruling over and caring for the world. Therefore, any 'headship' within the marriage is to be held in tension with the undoubted equality of man and woman before God.

In this context, it is the husband who usually has greater physical power, and often has greater financial power. Greater power entails greater responsibility, and we find that it is the husband who is instructed, at some length, to care for his wife as Christ cares for his church. And in doing so, that she be enabled to fulfil her potential as a woman of God. A high calling for him indeed!

And we find that the wife, who is even more vulnerable when pregnant and/or caring for children is, according to God, entitled to a husband who will love and protect and provide for her, as Christ loves, protects and provides for his Church. This is a daunting responsibility for any husband, and worthy of a wife's respect.

Your own reading

Each life journey is unique. The circumstances in which we grew up and the choices we have made, or that have been made for us are ours alone. God has not missed one step we have taken, and he knows exactly what he wants to say to each of us through his Word. Therefore, before we read a commentary or check out the notes at the bottom of the pages of our study bibles, we read, and reread the text. And then wait to hear the voice of the Holy Spirit speak through it into our hearts and minds concerning our own situation. We might be prompted to ask questions or be shown things we had not noticed before which we can go on to explore.

Perhaps we will find ourselves questioning previously held understandings of familiar scriptures. If what we have formerly assumed to be true is not firmly upheld by a careful reading of the text, we can have the confidence to ask God for further enlightenment, and the courage to stand on the truths that he shows us.

This does not mean that we can make any text say anything we want. It does mean that by reading God's Word in reverent submission to him, and applying what we learn to our lives, we just never know what might happen. Along the way we will also discover that we can never plumb the depths of wisdom contained in the Bible.

A WORD ABOUT REFERENCES TO GOD

A personal reflection – 2006

I read through the prologue of N.T. Wright's book, *The LORD and His Prayer*, OK, but then crunched to a halt. He writes: *'We want it* [to learn and grow in prayer] *because we know, in our heart of hearts, that we want the living God. We want to know him; we want to love him. We want to be able truly to call him Father'*.[2]

So, this is the foundation of a desire to pray—that we want to be able to know and relate to God as Father? Well I'm stuck right at the beginning. I don't know that I do yearn to relate to God as Father. Why?

I have no experience of what it means to be fathered, either by my biological father or anybody else. Moreover, the experience I do have of a man in that role in my life is a big negative. So not only no good example, but also a very bad example.

---
2   N.T.Wright, The Lord and His Prayer, 1.

> My initial response is "No, No No! I don't want to be able truly to call him Father."

I fully appreciate that many, many survivors struggle with the concept of God as father because of the experiences they have been through. I did so myself. Is this how we are supposed to refer to God? Can it be that we are obliged to do so?

It is interesting to note that no one, from the beginning of time, who worshiped God, referred to him as father until invited to do so by Jesus (Mt 6:1–18). God did occasionally refer to himself as "father" in the Old Testament (Jer 31:9), but the Israelites themselves did not. In fact, the Israelites didn't necessarily even speak his name at all, deeming it to be too holy to be spoken. Instead they preferred to use the term "Lord" or "Adonai." It was Jesus' radical use of the term "father" that led the way for Christians today to call God by that name, and to understand their relationship with him in this way.

So it seems we have permission to relate to God as father now, and are indeed invited to do so. But it is also possible to relate to him without using this terminology, or thinking of him in these terms, because this is what the characters of the Old Testament did for millennia before Christ.

What about the New Testament? The biblical commentator J. Ramsay Michaels notes that in the final book of the NT, John, the writer of *Revelation*, never refers to God as father. Michaels writes:

> Some modern readers of the Bible are no more ready than John was to call God 'Father'. They include feminists for whom the term carries too many implications of male domination, as well as numberless men and women

for whom the notion that God resembles their human fathers destroys all possibility of trusting God. The horror of child abuse and the void created by hundreds of thousands of absent or unknown fathers in our society has made the very term father problematic for many, both inside and outside the church. For them, the fatherhood of God belongs not to the present but to a future they are not ready even to imagine… If they are Christians, their God is not yet the 'Abba' of Paul's letters, but 'the Lord God' of the book of Revelation, the Alpha and the Omega… who is, and who was, and who is to come, the Almighty'… But Jesus and his angels draw near on almost every page…[3]

And so it is that many men and women readily relate to Jesus, as God, but hesitate to embrace the Lord God Almighty, Jesus' father, as their own. For this reason, I have made every effort to minimise my use of the term "father" in relation to God. I hope I have used it only where it is relevant to the particular teaching or study under discussion.

But does this mean I should avoid at all costs referring to God as being in any way male? Should I not use terms for God that have no reference to gender? Scripture tells us that God's nature embraces all gender characteristics, both male and female. These allusions help us to understand the nature of God in language we can understand. But this does not mean that God is limited in any way to a gender. God is in fact far beyond being classified in the human terms of male and female.

However, throughout the Old Testament the psalmists and

---

3 J. Ramsey Michaels, Revelation, 55

prophets, when talking about God refer to God as "he" and "him" (Ps 2:5; Is 6:11). And so it would seem that in order to help us understand a measure of his nature, in terms we can relate to, this is how God has chosen to try and communicate himself to us. And if this is God's choice, it must be for very good reasons.

The ultimate revelation of God to humankind is, of course, found in Jesus Christ, "the reflection of God's glory and the exact imprint of God's very being" (Heb 1:3). And Jesus was undoubtedly a man. If I were to try to 'de-gender' my image of God, would I need to 'de-gender' Jesus too?

This would make nonsense his ministry to us. For as a man who lived a sinless life, he freed us from the consequences of the actions of the first man, Adam. "The sin of this one man, Adam, caused death to rule over us, but all who receive God's wonderful, gracious gift of righteousness will live in triumph over sin and death through this one man, Jesus Christ" (Rom 5:17 NLT).

Some Christians do choose to avoid using gendered references to God, wherever possible, for very good reasons. However, for the reasons given above, and for reasons of simplicity, I have chosen to refer to God in these studies as 'him' and 'he' and very occasionally 'Father'.

SECTION ONE: ABOUT GOD

STUDY 1: GOD'S GRIEF

> "In the beginning, God created the heavens and the earth...God saw all that he had made, and it was very good"
> (Gen 1:31)

In the beginning it was very good. It is hard for us to imagine what this "very good" might have looked and smelt and tasted like before humankind were appointed stewards of it all. Perhaps deep in a rain forest we might be given an inkling of its original grandeur, beauty and complexity. Scripture tells us that God created it all for humankind to enjoy, and for him to enjoy humankind. If you have read *What About Yourselves* in the *Introduction*, you will know that unfortunately humankind decided to go about things their own way, independent of their creator. And that the world can no longer be considered to be "very good." It is neither "very good" environmentally, nor "very good" as regards how people are getting along with each other and with God on his planet.

Perhaps we are hoping that at some time in the near future people will get their act together and start fixing the problems by brokering peace between warring nations and by stopping pollution. If we all pull together, maybe we can sort it out? However, with negative news from all over the world constantly streaming through our digital devices, it seems an increasingly unlikely outcome, even here in Australia.

Even so, many argue, with good reason, that this is the best country in the world in which to live—I thought so myself when I migrated here more than half a lifetime ago. A job, good pay, clean air to breathe, sun, sand and surf. Really bad things happen overseas in other countries don't they? War, famine, slavery, catastrophic earthquakes and tsunamis. We become numb to the shocking images portrayed on the news day after day and are tempted to feel secure from such events—we will do our bit to help of course—but here: no worries.

A closer look at the local news, however, readily reveals that even in this 'lucky country' it is not all that good for many people. People are murdered here, children are offended against by those who should have a care for them.[1] Young women—and men—trapped by their circumstances, are prostituted by numberless, faceless clients. Mothers try to escape with their children from domestic violence and often risk being murdered in the process.[2] Many people are poor, homeless, mentally ill, or lonely. Many try to dull their pain with drugs. Many give up.

---

1   A Royal Commission into child sexual abuse within institutions in Australia was ordered in 2013 by the then Prime Minister Julia Gillard. This brought responses from thousands and thousands of people across the country who had been sexually abused as children.

2   The Australian Institute for Health and Welfare report *Family, domestic and sexual violence in Australia, 2018* states that one woman a week and one man a month was killed by their current or previous partner in the years of 2013 and 2014, 68.

HOW DOES THIS AFFECT GOD?

We will explore his character more fully in Study 2, but first of all, how do you think this affects God? A key clue to God's response to what has happened is to be found only six chapters into the first book of the Bible. Genesis 6:5-6 tell us "The LORD saw that the wickedness of humankind was great in the earth, and that every inclination of the thoughts of their hearts was only evil continually. And the LORD was sorry that he had made humankind on the earth, and it grieved him to his heart." This can also be translated to mean that God's heart was broken. And his heart was broken principally because people were being violent toward each other. This was not the way things were meant to be. And this is not the way things are meant to be now.

All the violence would not have been a problem for God if he didn't care deeply about people, but he did. And he had planned to have enjoyed loving relationship with every one of those individuals. But they had turned away from him and turned on each other. We can only wonder as to why on earth God chose to persevere with the human race when he knew how much pain it would cause him.

Later in the unfolding story of God and humankind, he wrote down a list of instructions as to how human beings should behave toward God and toward each other (Ex 20:1-17). This could be considered to be a type of 'Maker's Manual' on how to behave as a decent human being. It gives a glimpse of what he had originally intended for humankind. This list of ten basic instructions laid down the rules which, if obeyed, would make things more comfortable for everyone here on earth until the time was right for God to fulfil his plan to resolve the problem of sin, once and for all. This was done through the sending of his son, Jesus Christ.

In this list of ten commandments, God describes himself as a jealous God, who will punish sinners. For us, this is hard to understand. We tend to judge people by our own standards, and jealousy and anger are negative emotions that don't sit well with our image of a loving God. However, there is such a thing as righteous anger, expressed for good reasons. We have probably all been on the receiving end of some righteous anger from parents or teachers when we have done something that might endanger ourselves or someone else.

There is also a righteous jealousy, as expressed by a God who has such a passionate love for us that he wants our very best for each and every one of us. This type of love is expressed in Song of Songs 8:6–7: "Place me like a seal over your heart, like a seal on your arm; for love is as strong as death, its jealousy unyielding as the grave. It burns like blazing fire, like a mighty flame. Many waters cannot quench love; rivers cannot wash it away. If one were to give all the wealth of his house for love, it would be utterly scorned" (NIV). This is the kind of love that compelled God to send his one and only Son, the dearest treasure of his heart, on a supremely difficult and dangerous mission to earth: To rescue us and to make restoration of relationship with God possible.

Of all people that suffer at the hands of others, God's heart is particularly for those with less power—those who cannot defend themselves or cannot provide for themselves. In most relationships it is usual to find that one person has more power than the other. It may be that one person is smarter, or physically stronger, or has more money or social standing. Perhaps they know something that gives them leverage. Maybe they belong to a gang of like-minded individuals. Maybe they have authority over the other person, and therefore have power to give or withhold accordingly. Those with debilitating illness, those who are elderly and frail, those with no family or friends for support, those who are not so worldly-wise, or who are poor or without a voice can be 'easy pickings' if the power is misused.

We are made in God's image, and we are supposed to have God's heart for the same things that he is passionate about. Therefore, it is no surprise to find that Scripture is peppered by commandments to care for such people. These include widows and orphans, the poor, the downtrodden, the enslaved and the landless who have no means of growing food for themselves. We do not always do this, and therefore God has much to grieve about, because the breadth and depth of suffering throughout the world is immeasurable. However, not one bit of it escapes his notice. This would be unthinkable! I often wonder how God copes with never choosing to close his eyes to this suffering. I can flip channels on the TV, or turn the pages of the newspaper because I can't cope with seeing all the suffering, particularly that of little children, but God endures seeing it all.

THE SCALE OF THE TRAGEDY

The statistics for abuse that appear in research study after research study are staggering, and yet it is something that is very rarely spoken of in church. An American pastor recounts the experience of being on jury duty involving a rape case. She sat through the questioning of over twenty-five potential jurors.[3] In each case the judge asked: "Have you, or any member of your family or a close friend, ever been the victim of a crime, including sexual assault?" Person after person after person answered "Yes." She put the figure for reported rape in the US at that time as one in three of every women in her lifetime, and one out of every five or six boys before they are eighteen, and one out of every fifteen to twenty men. This was over twenty years ago.[4]

In a home group study I led in my local church, the topic of sexual assault came up. I asked around the eight people of the group if they had any connection with anyone who had been violated in this way. Surprisingly, seven out of the eight people had either been assaulted themselves or knew close family or friends who had suffered in this way.

The damage done by such abuse is felt in body, mind, soul and spirit, resulting in a multiplicity of wounds in the survivor which can manifest in depression, poor self-esteem, self-blame, and unresolved grief over losses that are sometimes hard to identify. It can result in intense anger, hate, inability to trust, shame, feelings of powerlessness, hopelessness and despair. Forgiveness seems a world away. What does it even mean?

The degree of injury is multiplied when perpetrated

---

[3] Pamela Cooper-White, *The Cry of Tamar*, 79-80.

[4] Current Australian statistics as regards violent assault are documented in the AIHW report *Family, domestic and sexual violence in Australia 2018*.

against a child. If abuse occurs within the home, the place of nurture, there is no safe place for refuge. If the abuse involves incestuous sexual assault, every boundary that might be expected to protect the most vulnerable in society is violated. The devastation occasioned by any such action is immeasurable. How it must break God's heart to see such evil perpetrated against any human being, let alone a child.

Given that there are many, many other forms of abuse than sexual assault, it is sobering to realise that on any given Sunday morning, at least more than half of all the women, and a goodly percentage of the men, present in church will have suffered significant abuse in their lifetime. If you are not one of them, you will certainly know someone who is a survivor whether you are aware of it or not. What great grief this is to God. This is why his heart was broken.

The ramifications of this abuse of power are complex and far-reaching. He made us to be social creatures, to enjoy each other's company. He said, "It is not good for man to be alone" (Gen 2:18). It is in relationship that we discover our own identity and express our own personalities. It is where we learn a robust sense of self which enables us to go out into the world with confidence in how we present ourselves to others. This is why the worst civil form of punishment is to put someone in solitary confinement, with no contact with other human beings.

As one Pastor explains, "We cannot survive and grow to maturity without personal contact with others who provide the context for relationships that touch the core of our being. We cannot exist as whole persons without relationships, and yet it is in relationships that we are most vulnerable to abuse and violence. Unfortunately, the more intimate a relationship is, the more vulnerable we are to being abused."⁵ As this same Pastor also affirms, "The most dangerous place for a woman is in an intimate relationship, and the most dangerous place for a child is in the home. So say those who work with victims of domestic violence. This is because most abuse takes place where there is the highest level of intimacy and personal contact."⁶

We are shocked. We can understand how vulnerable a woman may be in intimate relationship but we may exclaim, 'How can it be that the most dangerous place for a child is in the home?' and yet many of you reading this will know it to be true.

No one can blame anyone else if the rain falls, or the earth quakes. Or blame any specific person if the stock market plummets or a lightning strike starts a wildfire that rages through their property. Traumatic, injurious events happen and the blame cannot be pinned on any particular person. These events affect everyone in their path. But abuse targets those who cannot defend themselves for whatever reason.

When not only body and mind, but soul and spirit are harmed, how can a survivor of abuse recover their rightful sense of security and peace with themselves and the world? Pamela Cooper-White writes "... healing, if the restoring of the whole person is to take place, is a priestly work, involving nothing less than the anointing and revival of a crushed spirit, the reconsecration of a violated sacred temple."⁷ In other words, it must be a work of God. God therefore requires

---

5   Neil T. Anderson, *The Soul of Ministry*, 206.

6   Neil T. Anderson, *The Soul of Ministry*, 206.

7   Pamela Cooper-White, *The Cry of Tamar*, 152.

believing Christians to be involved in this mission of rescue and restoration.

More than one person has come to this study not thinking that it is relevant to them, only to discover that they themselves have been negatively impacted by the actions of someone else. They have been sinned against. Such abuse includes cursing and bullying, being stolen from, cheated, betrayed, assaulted, and even killed. And when relationships are compromised, a sense of self is damaged—'What is my worth?;' any sense of security is shattered—'How can I escape? How can I feel safe again?;' and questions about the character of God are raised—'If he is a so-called loving God, how could he let this happen?' Are these questions you yourself have asked at some time? Here in this study we are considering God's heart toward the powerless of the world.

QUESTIONS

Please be assured, there is no need at all for you to take part in any discussion on these matters unless you would like to do so and feel safe in sharing.

These questions are designed to prompt general thoughts on matters relevant to this topic. More in-depth discussion on particular issues will be possible later.

1. Read the notes concerning God's grief.

    a) Share any questions that have arisen in response to reading the notes.

    b) Share any thoughts or experiences that might be helpful to the group.

    c) Do you think God is feeling or has felt any grief about your situation, or that of people you know who have suffered at the hands of others?

2. God's commandments to humankind provide the basis for living a happy and peaceful life in community.

    - Read Exodus 20:1–17; Deuteronomy 6:4–5; Leviticus 19:18; and Mark 12:30–31.

    a) How many of the ten commandments in the Exodus

reading refer to relationship, either with God or with other people?

    b) Which relationship is spoken of first? Why do you think this might be?

    c) Jesus summarised the ten commandments into his statement in Mark 12. What do you understand about you yourself loving God? How well do you love yourself?

3. God feels very strongly about the violence that happens in the world.
   - Read Genesis 6:5–6, 11–13; and Psalm 11:5–7.

   a) Identify two different emotions God is said to experience concerning the wickedness evident on the earth at that time.

   b) What does the Bible tell us is God's attitude toward people who love to use violence?

   c) What does he say he will do to them, and why?

   d) Does this surprise you? Why or why not?

4. During a very dark time in Israel's history, the Hebrew people had strayed so far from God's ways of doing things that they had adopted the pagan practices of the original inhabitants of Canaan. This involved all kinds of lewd behaviour and in their worship of the god Molech they were burning their babies and children alive as a sacrifice.
   - Read Jeremiah 7:30–34; and 2 Kings 22:8, 11–13; 23:10.

a) What impact does this practice seem to have had on God?

b) How do *you* think God should deal with people who sacrifice their children in order to curry favour with a god of their own imagination?

c) Josiah was one of the good kings of Judah. What was it that opened his eyes to the evil that was going on, and impelled him to do something about it?

5. Scripture tells us how God expects us to act and how he will act toward those who disobey him.

- Read Psalm 72:1–4, 12–14; 146:5–9; and Jeremiah 5:26–29.

a) Psalm 72 is a prayer for the king of Israel. The king has all power in his kingdom. How is God expecting the king to use this power?

b) Psalm 146 is sung in praise of God. For whom is God showing particular concern?

c) What does this tell you about God's character and God's heart?

d) What does God say he will do to those who do not behave rightly to the poor and needy, and how does this make you feel?

6. Abuse of power can take many forms and is such an everyday occurrence within many homes, schools and workplaces that it may seem like normal behaviour. The injury may be felt in any combination of body, soul, mind and spirit.

- The 'Dart Board' diagram (on page 32) outlines a number of examples of abuse that may be used against different aspects of their target person. Any or all aspects of a person's identity may be affected.
- The specific forms which the abuse takes, for any individual, will depend on a number of different factors, some of which are listed below the diagram.

a) Take some time to study the 'Dart Board' diagram.

b) Identify which aspects of your personhood have been impacted by abuse, and what form it has taken.

c) Consider what resources you had, or have, in order to withstand the abuse, or avoid it, or escape from it.

d) Share any of your reflections with the group, if appropriate.

This series of studies aims to help expose the harm done to you, engage God's help in healing the hurts sustained, and establish you in relationship with the living God who has always, and will always love you unconditionally.

Figure 1.1 Dart Board diagram of abusive behaviours

Any or all of these aspects of personhood may be targeted by the offender.

How this plays out for a particular individual who is targeted will depend on many factors.

For example:
- Age
- Gender
- Religion
- Culture
- Location: Whether at home, work, school, play or in the community
- Relationship with the abuser
- Degree of opportunity/access
- Degree of isolation of the target
- Sense of self-worth of the target
- Level of secrecy involved
- Support network of the target
- Whether the abuser works singly, in a group, a gang, a family or a larger network.
- Whether the abuse is via electronic media:
    - There is potential for target-specific secrecy online, or via text.
    - There is potential for global exposure via social media.

STUDY 2: BEING GOD

> "Some children were brought to Jesus so he could lay his hands on them and pray for them. The disciples told them not to bother him. But Jesus said, 'Let the children come to me. Don't stop them! For the Kingdom of heaven belongs to such as these.' And he put his hands on their heads and blessed them before he left"
> (Mt 19:13-15 NLT)

"Jesus loves the little children, all the children of the world." So began an old hymn we used to sing in Sunday School when I was a child. Jesus said we needed to turn from our sins and humble ourselves like a little child if we wanted to enter the kingdom of heaven. Indeed, he cursed anyone who caused a child to lose their faith (Mt 18:6–7). Children were seen to hold a very special place in Jesus' heart. I came to better understand why when studying Psalm 139, where we are told that God pre-thought up each one of us, and "knitted us together in our mother's womb." We were God's children before ever we arrived in our earthly families.

Shortly after becoming a believer, I marked in the margin of my Bible, at Psalm 139:13, the surprised revelation "God is my Father." I came to understand that although I had been born in the normal way, with a mother and father, I had in fact been gifted to my earthly parents by God, for them to care for me and raise me. It was always his hope that I return, of my own choice, to be gathered back up into God's heart from which I had originated. That is why Jesus was sent into this world.

As we watch children growing up, we marvel at their innocence and their trusting nature. It is a delight to watch their exploration of the world and see things afresh, as if through their eyes. Who would have thought a delicate green leaf could emerge from a stiff brown twig?! A marvel! However just as this trusting nature is a delight to most adults and is treated with the respect it deserves, it also renders a child vulnerable to abuse and all too soon the infant acquires a knowledge of good and evil and their innocence is no more.

No wonder Scripture abounds with instructions to care for the orphans. How would we feel if we were to give our precious children into the care of people who didn't value them, didn't care for them at all, or who used them for their own selfish ends? For many if not most of those who were abused as children within their family, it may be a lifetime's work to re-learn the innocent confidence they were born with, and be enabled to return to God, trust in his love, and rest in his embrace as a humble child. For many it is, understandably, impossible.

How can a child whose trust has been betrayed and whose innocence has been violated ever be put back together again? We carry these wounds into adulthood. Can they ever be healed? Part of the answer to these questions can be found, not only in God's character, which is revealed in what has been done in and through Christ. But also in his nature, his being, the sort of living entity that he is. And God, in his goodness toward us, has not left us guessing as to his nature.

WHAT HAS HE TOLD US?

Considering creation

Scripture tells us that we can know what God is like because he reveals himself to us, firstly through his creation. "Ever since the creation of the world his eternal power and divine nature, invisible though they are, have been understood and seen through the things he has made. So they are without excuse" (Rom 1:20). Psalm 19 tells us that the heavens themselves are communicating to the whole world, in soundless voice, the handiwork of God (Ps 19:1-4). Among many other qualities, the wisdom, knowledge and sheer power necessary for such feats are evident in his creation, not to mention his magnificent detailed artistry.

Considering the Bible

Secondly, he reveals himself through his written Word, the Bible, which is the story of the relationship between God and humankind. Throughout the entire dramatic chequered history of the Hebrew people, the word of God has been faithfully passed on down the generations. What Moses wrote thousands of years ago, we can read today. What those who witnessed Jesus' life and ministry recorded in the gospels, we can read today. And what the Apostle Paul wrote in his letters to the infant church nearly two thousand years ago, we can read today.

The existence of the Bible itself tells us that we have a God who is reaching out to us, wanting to communicate himself to us. To someone who has felt rejected by family, or community, and feels worthless and alone, this may seem amazing.

And it is written not as a list of 'Do's and Don'ts,' but as story. As we identify with the heroes and heroines, villains and rogues, as well as the ordinary folk whose lives are recorded in this magnificent, true story, we are enabled to explore the nature and character of God. And we can wonder about how he is, even now, working in *our* lives.

Not only has God recorded his thoughts toward us, he has included our thoughts toward him. As we read the psalms, we hear and can identify with the voices of people who have suffered and sinned and argued with God, just as we have. How gracious of God to include our voices in his Word, giving us permission to voice just the same feelings to him. We learn that he cannot be shocked and will not take offence.

Considering Jesus Christ

Thirdly, he reveals himself through Jesus Christ. The Apostle John opens his account of Jesus' life and works by explaining that Christ existed from the beginning of time— "In the beginning was the Word, and the Word was with God, and the Word was God. He was in the beginning with God" (Jn 1:1). And that Christ was active in the creation of the world— "All things came into being through him, and without him not one thing came into being" (Jn 1:3). And that he came down from heaven to live among us as a fully human, fully divine Being— "And the Word became flesh and lived among us, ... full of grace and truth" (Jn 1:14). As such, his earthly form exactly represented God to us (Heb 1:1–3).

If the Bible—the Word of God—is all about God, Jesus is the embodiment of that truth. In effect, if we want to understand God as fully as we can, we look to Jesus who is "the image of the invisible God" (Col 1:15). What clearer picture could we have of the nature of God, than to have him presented to us as a fellow human being. We will explore more concerning Jesus Christ and his ministry toward us in studies 4 and 5 in this section.

GETTING OUR HEAD AROUND GOD

In the previous study, we considered how our suffering has impacted God. Here, in this study, we are considering how some of the things that are true about God's nature, his attributes, impact us. Only with a right idea of God can we lay a foundation for how we might usefully respond to him.

For example, if we have the idea that God is ready to strike us down when we think we have done something wrong, our attitude toward him is going to be one of fear. And we are going to be tempted to think we brought these terrible things upon ourselves. How different is our response to him when we understand that he is broken-hearted over what was done to us, and wants to rescue and restore us? It is quite a task we have before us. How can our human minds comprehend God, using human thoughts and human words, without risking reducing him to human size? But being mindful of this pitfall, we must make some attempt.

We may be familiar with the attributes of God such as holiness, justice, goodness, love, faithfulness and mercy, which determine how God acts. The Psalms are full of praise for these characteristics (for example Ps 145). Also, Scripture tells us his nature is eternal, infinite, unchanging, all-powerful and all-knowing (Job 37–39; Ps 102:26–27). All of these attributes are true facts concerning God's nature. There may, of course, be other attributes that God has not communicated to us, which we know nothing about.

However, the attributes that we know, and in some measure understand, all act together in God because they are who he is. For us it seems we can choose whether we will dispense mercy or justice toward our children. That is, will we let them off for being disobedient, or will we require them to feel the full effects of their behaviour? However, God can do no other than be merciful. He can do no other than enact justice. He can do no other than love. All of these, all the time. Because that is who he is. He does not have to choose between being just or merciful. Both always act together.

As A. W. Tozer, a well-known and well-loved theologian tries to explain, "All that God is must accord with all that God does. Justice must be present in mercy, and love in judgment. And so with all attributes."[1] Our minds struggle to grasp the unknowable! When trying to fathom the being of God, perhaps more helpfully Tozer, using the attribute of love as an example writes, "His love is the way God is, and when he loves he is simply being himself."[2]

How may understanding God's attributes help survivors?

Source of life

Scripture tells us that God is the source of all life on the planet (Gen 1). And therefore, he is the source of *my* life too. I came

---

[1] A. W. Tozer, *The Knowledge of the Holy*, 107.

[2] A. W. Tozer, *The Knowledge of the Holy*, 29.

into being because God gave me life. At the beginning of this study I explained that I discovered God thought me up, and then knitted me together in my mother's womb (Ps 139:13). The Psalm speaks of the loving tender care of God for the baby he is creating. And it is the same for each one of us. It means that each one of us is unique, and each one of us has great value in God's eyes.

We are also told that God himself sustains us (Ps 54:4). We don't keep standing on our two feet except that God enables us to do so. No matter what anyone else may say or do to us, we are here because God wants us to be here, because he loves us.

Eternal

If we consider God's eternal nature, we can ask ourselves, 'Do we think this life has sold us short?' When abused at any age the repercussions can resonate throughout the rest of our lives. Did we miss out on stuff we felt we should have had, relationships we should have enjoyed, or living conditions we felt entitled to?

We can be comforted by knowing that God has his own plans for us, while we have breath—"plans for your welfare and not for harm, to give you a future with hope" (Jer 29:11). We also know that Jesus has good works for us to do, which he has already prepared for us (Eph 2:10). So we know no matter what has happened, God plans to make the very best out of our earthly lives, whether long or short. However, we also know, that these few years are just the preamble to eternal life with God, where all our tears will be wiped away, and where we can enjoy heaven, forever, together with all other believers (Rev 7:17). We have a glorious future to look forward to. This life here on earth is not the main event.

Good, unchanging

It seems so obvious but nevertheless it needs to be stated that God is good. How terrible it would be if this were not the case! In addition, he will always remain so because he is the same yesterday, today and tomorrow (Heb 13:8). Whatever we learn of him that is true will never change. He is utterly dependable and faithful toward us. We can trust him. Scripture refers to him as a Rock, a sure foundation (Ps 62:1–2). What a comfort to those who have been deceived and betrayed. A measure of security in an insecure world.

Everywhere, all the time

God is everywhere, all the time. It is a great privilege and responsibility to raise a child. Parents who were themselves abused as children have sometimes gone to inordinate lengths to try to keep their own children safe. My own children were born before I became a believer and, like other parents, I had struggled to keep them safe every which way. However, I well remember the relief I felt when I realised that God was everywhere, all the time. And that he loved my children even more, and certainly better than ever I could. As I committed them into his care, I could rest in having done my best, leaving what I could not do, to him. However, this is not the only comfort to be derived from this aspect of God's Being.

Hasn't missed a thing

God sees everything and knows everything. As he lives outside of time, he can see its beginning and its end and everything in between. He is also holy and righteous. Secrecy is a noxious element of abusive relationships that is unloaded onto children in particular. Perpetrators use their power in different ways to silence their victim. "You are my special one. This is our little secret" whispers Daddy as he pleasures himself at his child's expense. "You mustn't tell anyone or you will get into terrible trouble" the young boy is told by his youth group leader. But as God is all-seeing and all-knowing, he has not missed one thing. He has not even blinked.

Justice will be done

I do not know how God copes with seeing absolutely everything all the time. It breaks his heart to see his little ones so cruelly betrayed. However, because he has not missed a thing, nothing, absolutely nothing will escape his judgment. This is a comfort to those whose cries have gone unheard and whose stories have been dismissed as unbelievable, for Scripture tells us they will be vindicated and justice will be done (Ps 135:14; Is 54:17).

How can we be sure justice will be enacted? God can do no other as he is holy, set apart, absolutely pure, with a purity which our human minds cannot begin to comprehend. It is not possible for sin-stained humanity to stand in his presence except in Christ. He is also righteous and cannot do other than see that justice is done. God will not be mocked.

Love

Operating powerfully with all other attributes is love. Love is of God. I remember as a brand-new believer asking my Christian friend if all the love in the world derived from God. Tozer explains love in light of other attributes of God. He writes, "We can know... that because God is self-existent, his love had no beginning; because he is eternal, his love can have no end; because he is infinite, it has no limit; because he is holy, it is the quintessence of all spotless purity; because he is immense, his love is an incomprehensibly vast, bottomless, shoreless sea before which we kneel in joyful silence…".[3]

However, this is just the start of a journey toward knowing God's love for us, for there must be a thousand different ways a heart can be broken. A broken heart requires a measure of healing before it can receive and hold the love that is poured into it. So perhaps, like me, as you progress in your walk with God, you keep on discovering the boundless nature of this love. And from time to time on the journey, you are surprised to find yourself embraced in a yet deeper place in God's loving heart.

It is a safe unexpected place to find ourselves if we have been trained up in self-preservation from childhood. Here we can rest, confident that we are being cared for by the One whose nature encompasses all the divine attributes. How could we know such a place existed? Yet this is a place we yearn to be, especially if the pattern of our lives has been dictated by fear. Perhaps at some point we will understand, like the Apostle John, that we have been led to a place where we no longer need to fear anything, because we manage to grasp not just that God loves perfectly, but that we ourselves, are perfectly loved (1 Jn 4:16–19).

---

[3] A. W. Tozer, *The Knowledge of the Holy*, 131.

QUESTIONS

1. God has reached out to us. Communicating himself to us through creation, through Scripture, and through his Son, Jesus Christ.

   - Read Psalm 19:1–4, 7–10; Romans 1:19–20; Hebrews 1:1–4; and 13:8.

   a) Do you see God's handiwork in creation? Why or why not?

   b) What does Psalm 19 tell us about God's law, and what it achieves (v 7-10)?

   c) God had no need to communicate with us at all. Why do you think he has gone to such trouble to reach out to us? What response do you think he is hoping for, from us?

   d) He finally sent his beloved Son, Jesus, not only to deal with our sins, but also to show us his own character in action. What do you learn about God's character from Jesus?

2. In 2 Corinthians 5:4, Paul speaks not of dying, but of being swallowed up by life. Scripture tells us we have a glorious future to look forward to.

- Read John 3:16–18; 6:47; Romans 8:18–25; Ephesians 1:11–14, 18; and Revelation 7:17.

a) Are you secure in the knowledge that you have been granted eternal life in Christ Jesus? Why or why not?

b) If you are secure in this knowledge, what difference does it make to your life here and now to know that you have heaven to look forward to?

c) Do you think eternal life in heaven will make up for all you have suffered in this earthly part of your life? Why or why not?

3. God does not miss a thing!
- Read Psalm 10:14–18; 33:13–15; 139:7–12; Luke 16:15; and Hebrews 4:12–13.

a) Do you mind that God never takes his eyes off you for even one moment?

b) Why do you think he watches you so intently?

c) Upright-looking people who are well thought of in their community are capable of abusing those they have power over, in private. This may be your situation. Did you share your story with anyone? Did people believe your story?

d) What comfort is it to you, if any, that their actions have not been hidden from God?

4. Nobody will get away with anything. People will be made accountable for their actions.

    - Read Psalm 57: 1–6; 89:14; 135:13–14; Jeremiah 2:34–35; and Revelation 21:1–8.

    a) Have you learnt anything new about God in reading these verses?

    b) Which text(s) particularly caught your attention, and why?

    c) Jesus spoke of two destinations hereafter: "eternal punishment" and "eternal life" (Mt 25:46). What are your thoughts concerning heaven and hell?

    d) Where do you think you will you be, and why?

5. To love someone does not always mean that we 'feel' loving toward them. It may involve experiencing a loving feeling or it may not, but it always involves action, because love compels good toward the loved one. It is self-giving. It is other-focused.

    - Read Romans 8: 38–39; 1 Corinthians 13:4–7; Ephesians 3:14–19; 1 John 4:7–12, and 18–19.

    a) Which verses tell us that God has taken the initiative in loving action?

    b) Do you believe God when he says he loves you? Why or why not? Do you have any doubts?

    c) How able are you to receive love? In other words, how comfortable are you with being on the receiving end of loving action? Explain your reasons.

d) How has the truth of God's love toward you changed your life, if at all?

Even having understood these things, still we puzzle to understand how all the good that God seeks to sow into our lives is of any account as we ask, "Why did he allow it in the first place!?" This foundational question is of such importance to survivors that the whole of the following study, is devoted to considering the sovereignty of God.

STUDY 3: GOD'S SOVEREIGNTY

God is supposed to be in charge, is he? As we boil with impotent rage against the injustice and the unfairness of what was done to us, we query the sovereignty of God. We cry out: 'What sort of a being are you that you can let this happen?' 'How can I put my trust in a God like that?' 'How can I even believe in a God like that?' These are the sorts of questions I have asked myself. I would think most people who have been through awful circumstances at the hands of others have asked: 'Why didn't God prevent it?' 'If he loves me and has all power at his fingertips, why did he allow me to go through all that stuff?'

Perhaps we know our assailant and are very familiar with their ways and means. If so, then we have a human focus for our anger. Perhaps it is not so clear, and in the confusion of our helplessness and pain we may not know quite where to direct our rage. No matter what we understand about our human situation, sooner or later this rage will be directed toward God.

It might seem surprising, but these questions are actually borne of a belief that there is (or may be, or should be) a God who is sovereign. One who is ruling over his creation, and who is supposed to love us—otherwise we would not ask it. However, the difficulty of trying to envisage a good and loving God, together with the action of terrible evil in the world, has caused countless numbers of people to choose not to believe in God at all.

Perhaps it may help to put aside our rage against God for a moment and reframe the picture. Perhaps, instead of focusing on God and what we think he didn't do, we choose instead to consider the sin against us? Sin basically, is someone doing things their own way, often for their own ends, independently of God. We have all done it, with barely a thought. Our own sins may seem small and inconsequential, but how dreadful can they be?[1]

If you have been sinned against, you will have a measure of its wickedness. Even if you have not felt the full force of its ugliness, you will have seen the results of the worst of it in the news, day after day. We become so familiar with the turmoil in the world that we don't often stop to actually put ourselves in the place of the victims. It may well be that we cannot feel their distress unless we have actually experienced the cause of it. Or maybe we simply cannot afford to think too deeply about the whole matter.

What does God think about sin? As we discovered in the first study, the Bible is crystal clear on this. He abhors it. He can't stand it. He hates it. His heart was broken because of it, specifically because of what it did to the powerless of society. The whole story of Scripture is the story of God seeking to rescue and restore us from the effects of sin.

---

1 There are many references to appalling sin, especially in the OT. For example, see Judges 19.

WHAT IF WE HAVE CHOSEN NOT TO BELIEVE IN GOD?

For those who do not have faith in a sovereign God, sin is not an issue. Some adopt the concept of karma, according to which any supposed good you do in this world will eventually come back to bless you, and any harm you do will have the same effect, eventually. This is a neat self-regulatory concept for governing behaviour in which you feature as the director of your own fate. Hopefully, if you do not cause suffering, you yourself will not suffer either. Presumably if you do suffer, you must have brought it on yourself. If you do not think so, then others may think it for you.

For others, suffering can be seen to be the action of an impersonal Fate—"Stuff happens. Deal with it." However, many who do not consciously believe in God can be seen to think of Fate as having purpose, as if alive. How many times have we heard "Everything happens for a reason." I have heard this statement twice just this week on the television. In each case, the circumstances were dire. In the more serious case, a young man lay gravely injured on a hospital emergency department bed, his sister comforting him. They had grown apart which caused the sister to understand that this awful accident had happened so that they would be reunited.

This is a way of trying to understand a really bad situation in a positive light, but does everything—usually something bad—happen for a reason? The outcome for their relationship was positive, but was it decreed by some impersonal fate—or even by God—that it should happen this way?

HAVE WE GOT THE RIGHT IMAGE OF GOD?

On reflection, I have to say that this is the general idea I had adopted concerning my Christian faith. I used to say: "I hope I learn everything I need to through this trial because I don't want to have to do this lesson again." In other words, everything that happened in my life was brought about by God to teach me something. "He won't test you beyond what you can cope with" I was assured. This is even what I read in big fat theological books, so it must be true!—mustn't it?

One theologian writes: "Jesus, who, though he was without sin, yet "learned obedience through what he suffered" (Heb 5:8). He was made perfect through suffering (Heb 2:10). Therefore we should see all the hardship and suffering that comes to us in life as something that God brings to us to do us good, strengthening our trust in him and our obedience, and ultimately increasing our ability to glorify him."[2]

I wonder how you feel when you read this? If our lives are reasonably comfortable, it seems much safer to assume that the sovereign God does govern every detail of our lives. We feel a bit insecure if we think something could happen to us that God did not will. We will no doubt try to discover some reason why suffering has happened in someone else's life—after all, we don't want to make the same mistake and suffer the same consequences!

However, from my new perspective I was actually shocked when reflecting on this theologian's statement. I was thinking "Is this what a woman is to be told whose eye has been blackened and whose ribs have been broken by the man

---

2   Wayne Grudem, *Systematic Theology*, 812.

she loved so much she had married him?" Already possibly (wrongly) thinking she deserved what she got, she is to believe that God brought it to her, to teach her a lesson, for her good and his ultimate glory! If this is our theology it is no wonder so many people choose not to believe in this supposed God—one who allows and even wills all manner of terrible things to happen to people when he could very well, if he is indeed sovereign, have prevented them.

Vital as the role of academic theologians is to our understanding of God, their conclusions need to make sense in real life. Feinberg, a pastor and teacher, wrote his Master of Divinity thesis on Job—a man of suffering. Later he wrote his thesis for a second postgraduate degree on God's sovereignty and human freedom. Studies for his doctorate led to his book: *The Many Faces of Evil*. He has therefore studied evil and affliction in depth. But when it actually happened within his own family none of these intellectual answers were found to be of any help in the face of what he was now feeling.

He writes, "Why didn't all the years of study, reflection, and writing on the problem of evil help at this moment of personal crisis?" He continues, ... "People wrestling with evil, as I was, do not need an intellectual discourse on how to justify God's ways to man [sic] in light of what's happening [rather, it] is a problem about how someone experiencing affliction can live with this God who doesn't stop it."[3]

GOD IS NOT THE PROBLEM

I was not challenged to question my own idea of God's workings in my life until I was confronted with the need to

---

3   John S Feinberg, 'A Journey in Suffering' in *Suffering and the Goodness of God*, 219.

address all the abuse that happened in my childhood. Now however, when I see on the news the images of children suffering in a war zone, their family buried beneath rubble, I can clearly see that God did not will these events in this child's life. Contrary to the theology quoted earlier, God did not bring that suffering to those children in order to do them good, in order to strengthen their trust in him, and ultimately to increase their ability to glorify God. It is *people* who willed this suffering in this child's life. *People* are the culprits.

How can I be so sure? When I myself asked God the "Why did you allow it?" question and searched the Scriptures, I found the broken heart of God as to the wickedness of humankind—even to the sacrificing of their own children—in the Old Testament. And I found his answer to this question in the New Testament, in Jesus Christ. The God I love is manifest in Jesus Christ, who is the *exact* representation of God (Heb 1:3). If I want to know God's character, I need to look at Jesus to see it acted out. Jesus demonstrates to me the outworking of God's will on my behalf.

WHOSE 'WILL' WILL PREVAIL IN THE WORLD?

Scripture tells us God has a plan and a purpose for each individual (Jer 29:11). It tells us God can bring good out of all disastrous things that happen to us (Rom 8:28). But it does not mean that he willed those evil things in the first place. Surely if everything on earth happened because the sovereign God willed it, there would have been no need at all for Jesus to instruct his followers to daily pray, "Your will be done on earth as it is in heaven" (Mt 6:10). So why *isn't* God's will always being done on earth? Is he in charge or not?

The root of the issue is that God's will is not the only will at work in the world. In his sovereignty, God has chosen to give humankind their own free will. A.W.Tozer attempts to explain the apparent difficulty of God's will being done, at the same time as the free will of humankind being at work by likening the earth and its inhabitants to an ocean liner.[4] Let us say that the liner is going to sail from New York to Liverpool. That is fact; Liverpool is the fixed destination and the boat will get there. This represents the pre-determined will of God as expressed in all the prophecies. God has spoken, which will therefore happen no matter what. However, everyone on the boat as it travels is free to do whatever they please. This represents our own free choices and actions while on the journey of life. Thus, to believe in God's sovereignty and the free will of humanity is not necessarily a contradiction. Both may be possible.

So it is that we have free will to pursue a godly life, and free will to live selfishly. We have free will to pray God's will on earth into place—as Jesus instructed us to do daily—or free will to pursue our own ends, at other people's expense. Were we hurt by another person? How can God overrule their free will and not potentially overrule our free will, or indeed everyone's free will?—we may as well be robots. He has, however, instructed us to pray for God's will to be done. Are we willing to do this? Which 'will' will prevail?

SUFFERING AS A CHRISTIAN?

Do we think that once we have become believers we will be safe from suffering? Well, not necessarily. Jesus himself said

---

4   A. W. Tozer, *The Knowledge of the Holy*, 147.

that his followers would face persecution (Jn 16:33). This is reaffirmed in Paul's letter to Timothy: "Indeed, all who want to live a godly life in Christ Jesus will be persecuted" (2 Tim 3:12). This does not sound good! Yet the Apostle Peter instructs us that it is better to suffer for doing the right thing, rather than for doing the wrong thing. Suffering for doing the right thing is what Jesus did for us (1 Pet 2:19–23; 3:16–18). And Jesus promises us blessing, should this occur (Mt 5:11–12).

Jesus also taught that some of this suffering was the work of Satan (Lk 13:11-13). And that Jesus' ministry was, in part, to heal "all who were oppressed by the devil" (Acts 10:38) and to "destroy the works of the devil" (1 Jn 3:8), who is also "the one who has the power of death" (Heb 2:14). So Satan, too, has a will which is totally and utterly opposed to God. And Satan chooses to try to cause maximum pain and distress to the object of God's love—all humanity—because this is what will most hurt God.

However, many people who have suffered abuse assume that they are being punished by God for something, but they are not sure what it is they have done to deserve it.

Did I do something wrong?

Scripture tells us that God will discipline us if we need it—the sort of discipline used by a loving parent to train their child in knowing right from wrong (Heb 12). Discipline is an outworking of God's love for us, for our own good, to grow us up in holiness. Quite often this may simply involve being required to endure the consequences of our own persistent disobedience. If we drive over the speed limit, we cannot expect God to disable all the speed cameras! And the outcome of discipline will be "a quiet harvest of right living for those who are trained in this way" (Heb 12:11 NLT).

On the other hand, punishment is an outworking of God's judgment on the ungodly. We have all been "ungodly" at some time. Thus, both discipline and punishment may arise as a consequence of our own sin. So it is important to understand the difference, because the whole complex burden of suffering that is loaded onto a victim is often secured there by the victim themselves. Because they think they deserved it.

Is it my fault?

So how can we tell if we what we are experiencing is punishment? God always makes the reason for it clear to us. For example, six hundred years before Jesus was born, Jerusalem was left empty and in ruins because the Israelites had been disobedient to God. They could, however, see the justice of the punishment that happened to them. They had no excuse, because the consequences for any disobedience had been clearly listed in Moses' teachings (Deut 28). Sorrow for their sin would come later (Neh 1:4–9; Dan 9:11). God had wanted to bless them, but this was not to be. What grief this caused to God we can only guess at. But in the heart of the book of Lamentations—which is an expression of the Israelites' sorrow over what happened—we find written "For he does not willingly afflict or grieve anyone" (Lam 3:33).

We can be assured then, that if anyone is suffering on account of God's punishment they, too, will be left in no doubt as to what it is they have done wrong. And they will be able to recognise the justice of the outcomes. Hopefully, like the Israelites they will also recognise that God takes no joy in either the sin or its consequences.

A GOD OF LOVE?

How does judgment and punishment fit with our idea of a loving God? Well, we may expect God to express love, but we cannot deny his justice. He enacts both justice and love at the same time, because, as we discussed in the previous study, he can do no other. What if God never warned us when we were straying into sin? It would be like feeling no pain in our bodies in response to physical illness. We may then die because we do not know of the illness, nor seek a remedy. If we recognise and respond to the warning, we have time to make things right with God.

God's answer to our questions concerning sin and suffering

Nowhere in Jesus' ministry does he suggest that the suffering he encountered—and for which he provided healing—was for either discipline or punishment. In fact, he didn't seem to answer any of the "Why?" questions of the disciples on this matter. Instead, Jesus took the punishment for all of our sins in his own body, so that we could be free of it.

The New Testament also tells us that there is a spiritual battle going on which we are caught up in, one way or another. Rather than assuming everything has been willed by God, good and bad, we are challenged to consider that as Christians, we are to join in the ministry taught to us by Jesus. This includes participating in setting people free, in healing blindness, and broken hearts, and comforting those who mourn. Indeed, in bringing about the will of God on earth.

Pastor and theologian Gregory Boyd, in his book *Is God to Blame?*, concludes: "We ordinarily can't know why particular individuals suffer the way they do. But in the light of God's revelation in Christ, our assumption should be that their suffering is something we should oppose in the name of God rather than accepting it as coming from God… Instead of asking 'Who sinned?' we should ask, 'How can we bring glory to God in this situation?'"[5]

But even so, we simply do not understand everything in this matter. It seems that in all of this there is a nexus of "unknowing" concerning God's will and what actually happens in the world beyond which we, as humans, cannot explore. We are finite creatures, limited in intellect, imagination and knowledge. Like Job, there are times when we express "pain and protest, submission and hope"[6] until finally at some point, we acknowledge God's greater wisdom while still trusting in his character as revealed in Jesus Christ.

---

[5] Gregory A. Boyd, *Is God to Blame?*, 84.

[6] John Goldingay, *Job*, 210.

QUESTIONS

1. If you have been a follower of Christ for any length of time you have probably been given the following verses as promises to hold onto, or have spoken them out to someone else for encouragement.

    - Read Jeremiah 29:11; Romans 8:28; and 1 Cor 10:13.

    a) Have you ever been given any of these verses when you have been suffering in some way? If so, how did you react in that situation?

    b) Are there any other verses, or any other words of 'comfort' you have been given that you would like to share? How did you react to them?

    c) What help would you like to have received in your circumstances?

2. Thoughts concerning God's sovereignty and our own free will have driven discussion, if not heated debate, over thousands of years. Our own opinion underpins much of how we respond to God and to the reality of suffering in this world.

    - Read Proverbs 19:21; Isaiah 14:26–27; Matthew 6:10; 18:14; Luke 13:34; and John 6:40.

    a) What questions are raised for you concerning the

issue of God's sovereignty and our free will? Is he in charge or not?

b) What questions have you asked God concerning your own situation?

c) What answers, if any, have you been given, and are they enough explanation?

3. In the stories of the patriarchs in the Old Testament, Joseph was the favourite son of his father Jacob, and got on the wrong side of his ten older step-brothers. When the opportunity presented itself, they beat him up and sold him into slavery in a foreign country.

- Read Genesis 37:1–11, 17–28.

a) How many 'wills' were involved in the action to beat up and sell Joseph?

b) Considering the character of God as you understand it, do you think God caused the brothers to act in this way, or even would have wanted them to do so?

c) What sorts of trauma is Joseph experiencing as a result of this event?

d) Given that Joseph seemed to act rather self-importantly toward his brothers, do you think he got what he deserved? Why or why not?

e) Do you consider what happened to Joseph to be God's discipline? Or punishment? Or neither? Why or why not?

4. Later in Joseph's story he is wrongly accused of making advances toward his boss' wife, thrown into jail and

forgotten about. Even so he stayed true to God and eventually was released and made second only to Pharaoh in status in Egypt.

- Read Genesis 39:1–3, 19–23; 41:37–40; 50:14–21; and Romans 8:28.

    a) Are you surprised, given the unfairness of all the things that happened to him, that Joseph stayed true to God? Why or why not?

    b) Do you think it would have been difficult for Joseph to respond to his brothers as he did? Why or why not?

    c) At the end of the story, how did Joseph choose to understand the hand of God in his life?

    d) Are you able to share any part of your story where you can see that God has brought a measure of good out of really bad circumstances that happened in your life?

5. Many people who suffer abuse truly believe that they are being punished by God for something, and yet they cannot identify what it is they might be supposed to have done wrong.

    - Read Isaiah 53:3–12; Luke 23:13–25; John 12:44–47; Romans 8:1-4; Colossians 1:15; Hebrews 13:8.

        a) Have you ever thought that the abusive circumstances you might have found yourself in were designed by God for your punishment? If so, punishment for what?

        b) If there is no judgment by Jesus, there is no condemnation. If there is no condemnation, there is no punishment. If you have trusted in Jesus, what happened to the punishment for any sin you might have committed?

c) Do you still think God is punishing you? Why or why not?

d) Given the verses above, if you were to describe God to someone, how might you go about it?

In the remaining two studies of this section we will hopefully discover what God has done concerning our suffering, which enables us to trust him through the 'unknowing' concerning God's will, and hopefully find comfort and healing for our broken selves.

STUDY 4: GOD WITH US

Have you ever heard a dawn chorus? Have you ever woken somewhere quiet enough for you to hear the local birds sing and trill and warble their welcome to the new day? As the earth spins on its axis there is always a new arc of daylight moving across the globe, awakening the birds to their chorus of song. A spinning singing planet. And it is not only creatures of the air and land that make noise. Records show that in Tasmania, the Derwent River was at times so full of whales that their haunting songs would keep the early settlers awake at night. It makes me wonder what a noisy colourful bustling place the newly created world must have been like, with the skies black with flocks of birds, and the oceans teeming with shoals of fish, and forests and plains crammed full of all manner of land-living creatures. Life, life, life everywhere, created for the pinnacle of God's creation, humankind, to enjoy and to manage.

What went wrong? The tragic choice made by Adam and Eve in the garden of Eden brought death into Paradise, for they chose not to be accountable to the God who had given them life. This brought into existence a deep gulf between themselves and the source of their existence. They no longer enjoyed daily fellowship with their creator, God, but now hid from him, afraid of what he might say about their actions (Gen

3). Were they simply ashamed of themselves, or did they not trust God to continue loving them, just as before and to deal with them accordingly? What was God's response to their disobedience?

The entire story of the Bible is the answer to that question, but possibly the most often quoted Scripture, certainly of recent times must surely be from John's Gospel 3:16, "For God so loved the world that he gave his only Son, so that everyone who believes in him may not perish but may have eternal life." The Father and Son so loved the people of the world, that they both chose to go through with this mission.

So, God gave, and his Son Jesus crossed the gulf between heaven and earth. Here he lived a fully human life, and experienced all that being fully human meant, including the suffering, and the dying. Jesus, Immanuel—which means 'God with us'—lived among us. And he did it to accomplish what no other being in the universe could do—transfer our destiny from that of eternal death to eternal life. We can only imagine the cost of this mission for both of them.

GOD'S HEART

The Bible tells us that it is not God's will that any should go to eternal death—that they should perish (2 Pet 3:9). And it seems his heart was particularly for those who were suffering at the hands of others. In the gospel stories told by Jesus, it also seems that these are the ones most likely to respond to his invitation to inherit eternal life (Lk 14:15–24). The hope of a blissful future in heaven is much better news for the poor and sick of the earth, than the rich and healthy.

God's concern for the powerless, the widows, the orphans, those with no land to call their own, the dispossessed, the oppressed and the suffering, rings out throughout the pages of Scripture, in both the Old Testament and New Testament. The kings of Israel, the most powerful people in the land, were commanded to use their power for good, to defend the cause of the poor, give deliverance to the needy and crush the oppressor (Ps 72:1–4, 12–14).

It is these very people who were particularly on Jesus' heart as he announced his ministry in the synagogue in Nazareth, the town where he grew up. "The Spirit of the Lord is upon me, because he has anointed me to bring good news to the poor. He has sent me to proclaim release to the captives and recovery of sight to the blind, to let the oppressed go free, to proclaim the year of the Lord's favour" (Lk 4:18–19).

What was the cost to God in bringing about the rescue of humankind? We know of Jesus' suffering. We will discuss that shortly. But what of the cost to the Father? What, if anything, do we understand about that?

OUR IMAGE OF GOD

What are your thoughts about God, particularly about God the Father? This is a tricky topic, particularly for any who have suffered abuse at the hands of their fathers. However, we are considering here, not our experience of being parented, but our experience of being in that role ourselves—of loving someone, and caring for them as a parent. It is necessary to raise this question here because our own, personal ideas concerning God are vitally important. For as I mentioned previously (Study 2 Being God 'Getting our head around God'), what we understand about God and his character determines our response to him. If we have got God wrong, our faith will have an insecure foundation.

What words would you use to describe God the Father? The God of the Old Testament is surely a crotchety old man, with grey hair, a long beard and bolts of lightning in hand ready to hurl at people, isn't he? Whereas the God of the New Testament is clearly loving kindness itself—like Jesus? However, Tozer warns us that we can risk imagining what God is like and then act as if this image we have conjured up, from our mere human brains, is true.[1] He calls such a response uncompromisingly "idolatry"—as if we were worshipping a false image. This is why we must make every effort to understand, believe and act according to a right idea of God.

Have we been tempted to imagine that God has exactly the same character as our earthly father? This may be helpful if our father is a godly man, but often this is not the case; after all, how often do we fall short as parents? If our father is unpredictable, unloving, unjust, even violent, how are we to know that this is not the normal behaviour of a father? And are we going to respond to God as we did to him? And what if we were given no father-figure role model at all?

God the Parent

It is worth bearing in mind that God's image is borne by both men and women. "Male and female he created them" (Gen 1:27). All gender characteristics derive from God—where else could they come from? Although God is beyond the human concept of gender, Scripture informs us that God can and does fully parent us—mother us and father us. Being both a father to orphans and a mother who nurses her child, plays with it on her knee and comforts it (Ps 68:5; Is 66:10–13).

---

1   A. W. Tozer, *The Knowledge of the Holy*, 19.

What can we know of the cost to God, in sending his Son to earth? Do we need to be a parent in order to have some inkling of what this means? Perhaps parents who have had to send their children off to fight in foreign lands may have some idea. Perhaps families who have waved their loved ones off onto missionary ventures to unknown reaches of the earth have some idea. Will they accomplish their mission? Will they return safely? Will my heart be broken?

Love can be freely given and received, but its loss is very costly. The more love, the greater the potential cost. And God's love is infinite. I have to say I truly do not know what it meant for God, as a father who loves infinitely, to send his one and only Son on such a mission. However, I am a mother, and grandmother. Does that count?

The answer must be that my motherly and grandmotherly instincts are valid, but can give me only a tiny taste of what parenting may mean for God. Likewise, an earthly father cannot fully know God's father-heart for his children. On the other hand, if we have loved, we know enough, we have experienced enough, for our hearts to be able resonate with God's, concerning the potential cost of this love.

God the Son

It is a fact that people, certainly in Australia, are more than willing to help out if someone is afflicted by a natural disaster. There is ready sympathy for those who have been burnt out by a bush fire or caught up in a flood. The afflicted communities are inundated with clothing, food and many other provisions, and if the disasters are overseas, money is generously given.

However, things are different if a person is suffering in an abusive situation, because the onlooker finds himself or herself needing to take sides. There is no neutral ground. "Do I do nothing and in effect help the perpetrator, or do I weigh in and help the victim?" Either way, one or the other is helped. As Judith Herman explains, "It is very tempting to take the side of the perpetrator. All the perpetrator asks is that the bystander do nothing... The victim, on the contrary, asks the bystander to share the burden of pain..."[2]

This means, in effect, that a person can feel good about themselves in helping victims of natural disasters—this is their reward for helping. On the other hand, the 'reward' for helping a victim of abuse is to share their pain. This is what Jesus did.

It is an amazing truth that God allowed his beloved Son to be so vulnerable in this sin-sodden world. He didn't arrive fully grown, but went through all the stages of development any human being does. From pre-born embryo, to babyhood; he was a toddler and pre-schooler before embarking on his schooling in earnest. He was a teenager and a young adult. He has reached out to every one of us.

What Jesus did was not only to empathise with those who suffer, he actually entered into that suffering himself. In choosing the suffering, he fully identified with all the powerless in society. How could God send his precious Son as a vulnerable tiny baby into such an evil world? This was the price he chose to pay in order to win back to himself people who would choose to honour the fact that he was the living God who had created them.

---

2   Judith Herman, *Trauma and Recovery*, 7–8.

Jesus could have failed

Amazingly, and thankfully, in his suffering, Jesus never once sinned. He could have. In which case all would have been lost. But fortunately for us, he never did. Not once. He never retaliated, or even had one sinful thought concerning his tormentors (Heb 4:14–16). If we check out his life and death, we can find he was tempted in every which way to respond sinfully to those who abused him.

For Jesus, an apparently illegitimate birth into impoverished circumstances were swiftly followed by the flight of the family from their country, in fear for the life of the infant Jesus. Growing up learning a trade in a rural town seems a humble setting for the raising of the child who was to become the King of kings and Lord of lords, but so it was. And despite the fact that he was loved by many, he was also mobbed and hounded by crowds. He experienced weariness, and grief. He suffered much rejection by his own people, and was hated by the established religious leaders of the time.

During the trial and crucifixion his suffering included being subject to betrayal, abandonment, false accusation, injustice, and being mocked. It included assault, rejection, shame, scorn and ridicule, curse, torture, agony, thirst and utter aloneness. And he went through it all for love of us.

WE OURSELVES HAVE NO EXCUSE

It seems hardly fair, but survivors of abuse are not excused from sinful response. There is no leniency because someone has suffered so much. We cannot claim the nature of our upbringing or our later life experiences as an excuse for continuing to fall short of God's commandments. It is just as important for a survivor to choose to follow the guidelines given in Scripture as it is for anyone else to do so (and of course we all fall short of perfection). This is not only because being obedient to God is an outworking of our faith in God, but also because these are the guidelines which will keep us from falling into much trouble. They are for our good.

The fact that Jesus submitted to suffering as we do gives him authority to speak into our lives. As survivors we can't say "You don't know what it is like." He does. And he came through victorious. And because of what Jesus has done, we can come through suffering, victorious over sin too. It is as if he has reached down into the depths of the worst suffering that can happen to a person at the hands of another. He then gathers up those people in his arms and lifts them up and out of the darkness into the same victory over being sinned against that he himself has won. This enables us to experience life in all its fullness, free from the shame, guilt, grief, loneliness, unforgiveness and the many other bondages that have bound us for possibly a lifetime.

By God's magnificent grace, if we believe Jesus is who he says he is, and choose to accept what he has done for us, God chooses to see us "in Christ." Sinless, victorious, and very much alive. Forever.

A fuller account of the cost to Christ of going through with his mission is offered in Appendix 1. It is a personal reflection on Jesus' prayerful struggle in the Garden of Gethsemane, the night before the crucifixion.

The following Bible readings and questions will help to fill out an understanding of how Jesus has fully identified with all of our sufferings. He truly does know and care about each and every one of us.

Questions

His nature

1. The fact that Jesus is both fully human and fully divine differentiates Christianity from all other religions, cults and sects. Jesus is unique.
   - Read Luke 3:23, 38; John 1:1–5, 10–18; Philippians 2:6–8; Colossians 1:15–17; 1 John 4:1–3; and 2 John 7.

   a) What references can you find in these verses firstly to Jesus' divinity, and secondly to his humanity? Which verses (if any) are your favourite and why?

   b) What do you understand "the Word became flesh" to mean?

His birth

2. Read Matthew 1:18–25, 2:13–15, 19–23; Luke 1:38, 2:1–7, 15–24.

   a) What do you think family and friends might have thought about this pregnancy, and what might this have meant for Mary and Joseph?

   b) How did God affirm, comfort, encourage and/or provide for each of them during this time?

c) List all of the dangers to the baby Jesus that threatened his survival. How did God keep him safe?

Jesus was born an apparently illegitimate child to a young mother in a shed housing livestock. While still a baby, his life was in danger and his parents became refugees in a foreign culture. The two young pigeons given as sacrifice at Jesus' dedication were the offering given by a relatively poor family.

d) Do any of these circumstances resonate with you? If so, have you been enabled to see the hand of God at work to keep you safe and rescue you?

His childhood

3. Regardless of the difficulties of his babyhood, Jesus survived and apparently thrived. These few verses from the Gospel of Luke indicate he was healthy, intelligent, well liked, and well taught in the Jewish faith. Joseph was a carpenter, and Jesus would have learnt the skills of the trade, fashioning the wood of the trees he had originally created!

- Read Luke 2:39–52; Psalm 10:14, 17–18; Psalm 68:5; Ephesians 1:5.

a) Jesus seems to have enjoyed a happy childhood in a normal family life with brothers and sisters. Does this resonate with your childhood?

b) How might this childhood have stood him in good stead for his later ministry?

c) If you did not experience a good and happy childhood, what comfort do you find for your future, (if any) from the character of God and his promises in his Word?

His ministry years

4. Read Hebrews 12:2–3; and Zephaniah 3:17–18.

    a) In the Hebrews reading, what do you think was the "joy" set before him that drove his ministry endeavour?

    b) Do you consider that you bring God joy? Why or why not?

Jesus suffered rejection by his home-town community, and later, by a Gentile community.
- Read Mark 6:1–6; Luke 4:22–30; 8:34–39

    c) How did he respond to this rejection?

    d) How do you cope with rejection?

    e) What difference does it make to you, if any, to know that God welcomes you?

Jesus was misunderstood, plotted against and persecuted by the religious leaders.
- Read Matthew 12:9–14; 26:1–5; John 5:14–18; Psalm 57:2–6; and 139:1–6.

    f) Can you think of times when you have felt unheard, been misunderstood, or had your intentions misjudged? How did you feel? How did you respond?

    g) According to Psalm 57, how will God respond toward people who plot against you?

h) What difference does it make, if any, to know that God will have heard, listened to and understood you?

Despite all the challenges, Jesus persevered in his ministry to the needy.
- Read Matthew 4:23–25; 9:35–36; 15:29–31; Luke 13:34; and 19:41–44.

i) Do you consider yourself as one of the 'needy' to whom Jesus ministered? Why or why not?

j) When talking of his having been rejected, for whom did Jesus weep? Does this surprise you? Why or why not?

His death.

5. Jesus suffering came to a climax in the events leading up to and including his crucifixion. His suffering affected his whole being, body, mind, soul and spirit, and is particularly relevant to people who have suffered abuse of any kind.
    - The account of Jesus' betrayal, trial and crucifixion is quite long in each gospel. If you can, read Luke 22:39–71 and 23:1–49.

    a) All of the following abuses are suffered at some point by Jesus. See if you can identify when they occur. Betrayal; Abandonment; Mocking; Assault; False accusation; Injustice; Rejection; Shame; Scorn and Ridicule; Curse; Torture; Agony; Thirst.

    b) Did you note any others that have not been included here?

On the cross, just before he died, Jesus speaks out the words *"My God, my God, why have you forsaken me?"* from Psalm 22:1. The psalms are poetry, which puts into words emotions people are experiencing. This psalm, in particular, resonates with the crucifixion drama.

- Read Psalm 22; Hebrews 2:17–18; and 4:14–16.

    c) Does any part of this psalm resonate with your experience?

    d) Does any part of this psalm express how you felt at the time of the abuse?

    e) What does it mean to you, if anything, that Jesus voluntarily experienced this suffering?

For some, God as parent can be a challenge, if not an obstacle to faith. However, it can also be a source of great comfort to those who have grown up without the experience of having someone trustworthy, wise, loving and powerful providing for them and protecting them.[3]

---

3   I appreciate many people have problems with thinking of God in terms of father, or even male. Please see notes on 'A word about references to *God*' in the Introduction.

STUDY 5: MISSION ACCOMPLISHED?

When I first became acquainted with Jesus, I had just said to my Christian friend "I believe in God and I believe in the devil, and I'm on God's side. But I don't understand where this Jesus Christ fellow fits in." And moments later, I still didn't understand "where he fitted in," but I did know of his reality and I experienced his love for me. So the answer to my question could wait! However, I have since, of course, explored "where this Jesus Christ fellow fits in." And in the course of my journey of faith, I have come to learn something of what he accomplished through his incarnation. And I have been surprised at what I discovered.

What do you think God hoped to accomplish through the radical event of Jesus leaving heaven and coming to live on earth? Perhaps you have little idea, but if you are a regular church-goer you may say something like "He came to die for my sins, so I can go to heaven when I die." Or perhaps "To pay my debt (what I owe God because of my sin) and put me right with God." This is the message given Sunday after Sunday in Churches around the world, and it is very true. But it's not all.

Jesus' life on earth as a human being—his incarnation, ended in unimaginable suffering, followed by his death and resurrection. It looked like his mission had ended in failure at the cross, until he came through the event very much alive. What was achieved?[1]

Firstly, Jesus' resurrection demonstrated that, astonishingly, he had defeated death. How come death was defeated? Scripture tells us that death was the inevitable consequence of sin (Gen 2:17; Rom 6:23). And Jesus never sinned. Not once. Therefore death—the result of sin—couldn't 'hold' him, and he came right through death, very much alive.

Secondly, this means he was also victorious over sin. Jesus died in our place, innocent of any sin. Because of this, his own life blood that was shed at his crucifixion redeemed us from the sin that has so often directed our thoughts, speech and actions. This means that Jesus himself paid the debt we owe to God on account of our own personal rebellion against our creator (Rom.3:23–25; Eph.1:7).

And thirdly, he was also victorious over Satan. No longer could the devil claim us for his kingdom (Col.2:13–15; Eph.2:1–7; Heb.2:14–15). Satan had tried to kill Jesus before, when he was just a baby. And he had failed. Satan then had tried to tempt Jesus into doing things the devil's way—appealing to pride and ambition, which Satan himself knew all too well (Mt 4:1–11). And he had failed. And in orchestrating Jesus' death on the cross, he thought he had finally won the battle. Until the resurrection. What Satan had thought of as victory was a comprehensive defeat that led to an unimaginably far-reaching victory for all who would ever choose to believe in Jesus Christ from any nation on earth for all time.

And so, we find that the challenge usually given to non-

---

[1] It is not possible, in just a few short sentences, to communicate the scope of what Jesus accomplished through his crucifixion. These verses are given as starter points for your own further research. Whole books have been written on this topic. For example, Bible teacher John Stott's book, *The Cross of Christ*, provides detailed background teaching on all aspects of Jesus' victory at Calvary.

believers wherever they may be found is to put their trust in the Saviour, Jesus Christ, and ask for their sins to be forgiven. In doing so, they are restored to right relationship with God and can claim the victories listed above. However, as I explained in About Me in the Introduction, this is not necessarily the only way that people come into relationship with God. And as we will discover, Jesus' victories won by his death and resurrection are by no means the only accomplishments of his ministry.

THERE IS MORE?

When "the Word became flesh and dwelt among us" (Jn 1:14), we find that Jesus, having lived among us, accomplished more than these victories. For through his incarnation, Jesus showed us in flesh and blood, the heart of God toward us—his love and compassion for us, and his yearning to have relationship with us restored. And Jesus also modelled to us, not only God's character, but also perfect humanity. That is, Jesus has shown us, without fear of being misunderstood, how human beings were meant to behave toward God and toward each other.

Following on from this we come to realise that God's mission through Jesus Christ was not just to restore relationship between himself and individual men and women, boys and girls. His mission was also to restore relationships between people. And so we find it was not just to secure a glorious future for us, in heaven, with God, forever; his mission was to make a difference to our life here on earth too. Where there had been division, there was to be unity. Where there had been distress, there was to be peace. Where there had been rejection, there was to be found a place of acceptance and belonging. This is what we find in the records of Jesus' ministry on earth.

As we check out the gospel stories we discover, time and time again, that after ministering to people, Jesus reconnects them with their community. The woman at the well arrived alone, but was left in the centre of a newly formed group of believers (Jn 4). Blind Bartimaeus, when healed, was gathered up into the crowd of people following Jesus into Jerusalem (Mk 10:46–52). The healed lepers were sent to be checked by his local priest so that they could be deemed clean, and be allowed to rejoin their community (Mt.8:1-4; Lk 17:11–14). The demon-possessed gentile man of Gerasene, who had lived alone, out of his mind among the tombs, was told to go home and tell his friends how he had been healed (Mk 5:18–20). Sons and daughters who had died were restored to their families (Mk 5:35–43; Lk 7:11–15).

A LESSON FOR ME

In 2006 I visited Thailand as part of a team learning about Baptist missionary work in that country. In the north of Thailand, an effort had been made to work with the Thai government on behalf of orphans who had lost their parents to AIDS. Instead of building orphanages for these children, and therefore separating them from everything familiar, their grandparents were provided with the means of making a modest income. This was sufficient for these children to be raised in their home village among extended family and the friends they had grown up with. This is a beautiful example mirroring Jesus' concerns to maintain community.

On the other hand, there were children there who had been trafficked from Myanmar for the sex trade. There was no way for these children to be returned to their families, and an orphanage was, at that time, the only way to provide for these rescued children. All their photographs, and something of their background was displayed on a wall. I was deeply moved by reading their individual stories. I felt somewhat helpless. I, too, had suffered greatly, but I had a living relationship with God, who loved me. And I had access to professional help that many, many others do not. It was one of the motivations for writing this series of studies.

In our earthly lives, we each need a place of belonging where we are loved and valued for who we are. We need a place where we feel secure and can rejoice in life. We need a means of contributing to society so that we have purpose in what we do. And we need a future to look forward to. How did Jesus make provision for these needs to be met, for all believers? And why is this provision most especially needful for those who have suffered abuse?

THE ORIGINAL CAUSE OF THE PROBLEM

When sin severed Adam and Eve's relationship with God, not just death but great anxiety was experienced by humankind too. This is because a creature who has wilfully turned its back on its caring creator must fend for itself. If independence is chosen, the man or woman must make their own way in this world and manage as best they can to provide for their own needs.

The temptation was overwhelming for those with greater strength to secure for themselves what they thought they needed in order to survive, at the expense of those who were weaker. Thus, we find that within a few pages of the beginning of the Bible, wickedness and violence are so rampant that God says he was sorry he had ever created people, and his heart was broken (Gen.6:6).

Things have not changed. People still choose to do their own thing, independently of God. And many of those with the muscle power or the money or the status, trample all over the powerless in society, bullying, controlling, stealing, lying because they can, and because they do not acknowledge that they will answer to God for their actions.

For many of them, their actions are driven by their own insecurities. In some situations, a person may feel they need to control others in order to feel safe and provided for, instead of looking to the living God for their protection and provision. And in so doing, they destroy their relationships, whether within family, work, community or even country.

The result

And so it is that to suffer abuse can be very isolating. When asked how I coped with my childhood, my answer was found to be "I managed by myself." I was very lonely. Perhaps isolation can be felt because what has happened simply cannot be talked about for a variety of complex reasons, some of which are discussed in the second section of studies, About Ourselves. Or perhaps there is no 'safe' person with whom to share your story. This aspect of isolation is explored more fully in Study 10, Silence is golden?.

In other cases, families may have been broken up on account of domestic violence. Children may have been removed from their homes into government care. Because of bullying or other forms of abuse, people may have had to change jobs, or children their schools, which means starting relationships anew. On an international level, refugees have had to leave their own country often in fear for their lives. For some people, even becoming a believer means they have had to leave their family for fear of reprisals. What does Jesus provide that might help us in our isolation?

JESUS' PROVISION

Eyes opened

Possibly the first 'help' we experience is a reframed worldview. We come to see and understand the world differently. A key miracle in Jesus ministry was that he opened the eyes of the blind. This he did on a physical level many times, but more importantly he opened our eyes to understand spiritual truth about our situation in relation to God.

For me, it was as if I had been looking at a page of text upside down, quite unable to make any sense of what was written. Then the book was turned right way round and I could read it! Same pages, same writing, but entirely different understanding! I found that when Jesus came into my picture, although everything looked the same, visually, I understood it differently. And it all made wonderful sense! With this revelation my values changed, and a change in my behaviour inevitably followed.

For people who have been held captive by lies, this is welcome revelation. "I tell you the truth" occurs in the gospels nearly eighty times. Jesus also said, "I am the Way the Truth and the Life" (Jn 14:6). Our current society tells us that we can act according to our own version of truth. Whatever works for us, whatever makes us happy, as long as no one else is hurt by it, we can believe what we like. But Jesus secures our understanding in rock-solid, unchangeable truth. And this truth, he says "will make you free" (Jn 8:32).

With this new view of things, we can come to see that we

are also provided with a sense of belonging somewhere, be it family, community or kingdom. And as we find where we fit, not only should we discover our value as human beings, we should also discover we have something to offer others with whom we now rub shoulders—other believers. As valuable individuals we now have a place to belong, and something to contribute. Life has meaning and purpose.

Kingdom citizens

Scripture tells us Jesus came to establish his kingdom "on earth as it is in heaven" (Mt 5:10; Eph 2:19). This kingdom does not have a geographical location. Rather, it is a spiritual reality. We may have been lonely and dispossessed, but now we find ourselves accepted into the people of God. We belong somewhere. And we find ourselves with rights and responsibilities we did not have before. For when we choose to become citizens of any country, we pledge allegiance to its leader and agree to abide by its laws.

These laws provide the boundaries that dictate our behaviour. We find these laws of the Kingdom throughout Scripture and they are summarised by Jesus as loving God wholeheartedly, and loving others as we do ourselves: "On these two commandments hang all the law and the prophets" (Mt 22:34–40).

And a kingdom has a king. Therefore, as a Christian we also undertake to honour and support the leadership of the King of kings and to be loyal to his cause. So it is that being a citizen of a kingdom gives our lives focus and a clear idea of how we are expected to behave. This is for our own good, and to the glory of the King.

Community

Here within this kingdom we also discover community. At the beginning of time God had said "It is not good that the man should be alone" (Gen 2:18). And as I illustrated earlier, we discover that each time someone who is alone, or isolated is healed by Jesus, he re-establishes each of these individuals in their community. Being embraced by community is particularly important to those believers who have been banished from their family or community on account of coming to faith in Christ, or who have had to leave on account of other forms of abuse within the family.

Sometimes this community is referred to as the Body of Christ, within which we are all individually gifted to accomplish our various works in Christ. It is also sometimes referred to as a building, the Temple of God, his dwelling place, or as the household of God (Eph 2:19–22). Whichever imagery is used, Scripture tells us that in this community a person should find themselves loved and cared for by other believers, which includes receiving ministry for our wounds.

There will be some reading this who will be saying to themselves, or anyone else who may be listening, that church community was where they received their deepest hurts. This can, tragically, be the case. None of us are perfect, and we make many mistakes. We can operate out of our own hurts which have never been addressed. However, anyone can call themselves a Christian, and can attend church and be involved in ministry without truly being a believer at all. And a person can be deliberately predatory in a church environment, causing immeasurable damage not only to individual victims, but to the name of Jesus, and the reputation of his church. Nevertheless, despite these shortcomings, the church community is God's provision for us all. And if we followed Jesus' instructions to "love one another as I have loved you," we would make a better job of it (Jn 15:12).

Jesus taught his disciples, and therefore us, how to carry on his work of releasing those held captive spiritually, mentally or physically, so as to provide healing and restoration. And because we are all given gifts of the Holy Spirit, we should each discover our role within this community, and our means of contributing useful service (1 Cor 12).

Family

It is not only a Kingdom and, within it, a community that Jesus established but also a family. Because we are all considered children of God, we all share the same parent (Jn 1:12–13). Is this a blessing or more of a challenge? It is very true that you can choose your friends but you cannot choose your family. How wonderful it is when family works well! However, perhaps, like me, when you became a Christian you found yourself needing to get along with people you would not naturally have become friends with. And we no doubt find family members we have some difficulty relating to. Nevertheless, as fellow Christians we all have the same Holy Spirit indwelling us, and it is as if we all have the blood of Christ flowing in our veins. We are blood brothers and sisters in Christ.

Inheritance

There may be challenges, and there will hopefully be blessing to be found in this, but as with any family, we also find we have certain legal entitlements. On coming to faith, we are all—men and women—counted as sons of God. And as sons, or children, we are also heirs, with legal rights of inheritance. What is it that we inherit here and now, in our earthly life? We inherit all the covenant promises granted to Abraham, and all the other promises we find within the Bible. Wonderful entitlement indeed (Eph 1:5, 11–14)! "What no eye has seen, nor ear heard, nor the human heart conceived, what God has prepared for those who love him" (1Cor 2:9).

CHRIST'S BODY IN ACTION

The Body of Christ now extends around the world, and its function is to carry on accomplishing the things that Jesus did while on earth "and in fact will do greater things than these" (Jn 14:12). Who would have thought that God would entrust such a task to his wayward creatures? And yet this is both daunting responsibility and challenging adventure.

This first series of studies has been written to enable you to review your thoughts about God in light of Jesus' ministry, and consider whether these thoughts are to be affirmed, added to, or even corrected. Perhaps they have been challenged, possibly even changed. Hopefully whatever your journey, your thoughts about God form a firm foundation for your faith.

QUESTIONS

This topic is so large that it could rightly form a whole series of studies in its own right. The purpose of it here is not to provide in-depth study for each outcome, but to prompt us to review our previous thoughts about God, and what he has done for each one of us, and to consider whether those thoughts were both correct and anywhere near complete.

These outcomes all centre on the truth that God yearns for a living relationship with each individual one of us, for our own good and his great pleasure. Maybe you can think of some more?

1. Christ paid for our sin.
   - Read Genesis 2:16–17; 3:6–7; Isaiah 53:12; Matthew 26:26–28; Romans 3:23–24; and 1 Peter 2:24–25.

   a) What do you understand sin to be? How bad would you consider yours to be?

   b) What was supposed to happen to us on account of our sin?

   c) What did Christ do for us?

   d) Have you asked God to forgive your sins? If not, do you feel any need to do so?

2. Christ defeated death. Eternal life was gifted to us.
   - Read Job 19:25–26; John 3:16; 5:24; Romans 6:23; and 2 Cor 4:16–18.

   a) What did you think might happen to you after death, before you became a Christian?

   b) What do you believe now?

   c) Does the knowledge that in Christ you will live forever make any difference to how you view the life you live now on earth?

3. Christ defeated the devil.
   - Read Hebrews 2:14–15; and 1 John 3:8.

   a) Who or what do you understand the works of the devil to be?

   b) What experience do you have, if any, of victory over the works of the devil?

4. Christ demonstrated the heart and character of God toward us.
   - Read Colossians 1:15; Heb 1:1–4.

   a) Is there any difference in your own mind between how you see 'the invisible God' of Colossians, and how you see Jesus? If so, explain what that difference is.

   b) After reading these texts, do you think there should be any difference? Do you have difficulty with thinking of them as identical in character and heart toward you?

   c) Has your image of God the father of Jesus Christ been

adjusted in any way as you have completed this first series of study? If so, how?

5. Christ gave us his Holy Spirit, and communicated truth to us.
   - Read John 8:31–32, 14:6, 16–17; 16:12–13; 18:37; and 2 Corinthians 4:4–6.

   a) Have you ever experienced a 'light bulb' moment concerning God's truth?

   b) Do you have any experience you can share of God's truth setting you free?

6. Christ came to rescue people from the consequences of being sinned against.
   - Read Luke 4:16–19; Isaiah 61:1–2; Psalm 18:16–19; Psalm 72:4, 12–14; and 146:5–9.

   a) Which of these verses speaks most clearly to you in your situation?

   b) What do you think are God's thoughts about your situation?

   c) Christ also taught all his disciples how to help others who had been sinned against as an ongoing ministry. Are you involved in this ministry yet? If so, how?

7. Christ established his Kingdom.
   - Read Matthew 4:23; 5:3; Philippians 3:20; Colossians 1:13; Matthew 22:34–40; and John 15:12.

   a) What do you understand this heavenly kingdom to be?

b) What are the laws governing behaviour in this kingdom?

c) What do you think might be included in your entitlements and responsibilities as citizens of this kingdom?

8. Christ established community.

Please note: As explained above, anyone, and any community can call themselves Christian without necessarily actually being so. Or if they are truly Christian, they may not necessarily be behaving in line with God's will. If you do not feel welcome in such a community, or feel safe, or you feel you are unable to grow in your faith, bring your concerns to God. Ask him about possibly moving you to another Christian fellowship, because caring Christian community is what God has intended for you.
- Read Romans 12:4–8; 1 Corinthians 12:12–27; Ephesians 2:19–22; and 4:15–16.

a) Are you a member of a Christian fellowship where you feel you belong? If not, would you like to be. Why or why not?

b) What do you think are the gifts you have been given by the Holy Spirit?

c) What would you like to receive from a Christian fellowship, and what would you like to contribute?

9. Christ establishes family.
- Read John 1:10–13; Galatians 3:26–29; 4:4–7; Ephesians 1:5–6, 18–20; and Hebrews 2:10–13.

a) What does it mean to you to be legally adopted as a child of God?

b) If Jesus Christ is Son of God, King of kings, and a brother to believers, what is your status in this family? What does this mean to you?

c) What are some of the promises you have inherited that are particularly precious to you?

SECTION TWO: ABOUT OURSELVES

STUDY 6: WHAT'S IN A NAME?

A PERSONAL REFLECTION – 2006

Who can I trust?

For the purposes of argument, say I have broken my leg. It can be mended. Medical professionals, family and friends view the leg and consider the process of fixing it. The timeframe. The prognosis. The treatment. So would I. Objectively. Does it matter which doctor? Not really. It is after all, only my leg.

But for me, it is not my leg, it is my actual Self that is broken.

This is the part of me that is up for scrutiny, analysis, consideration, mending.

Why did it do this; behave that way; say such and such? What is the prognosis for this broken self? What is the timeline? When will it be mended? What is the process to be gone through? Will it be as good as new?

This is not a part of me. A leg. It is me, my Self. Profoundly private, hidden. Formed in utter seclusion.

Who is to be allowed a glimpse of 'Self'? Only those with whom you feel safe. Those who will care for 'self' as they should. Handle 'self' sensitively, reverently. Love 'self' with God's own love. Respect 'self'. Honour 'self'.

Can 'self' of another be viewed, or considered, objectively. Yes.

The very spirit/soul/essence of a person, that carries the image of God can be objectified.

Is that safe? No. Not at all. With no perceived connection, no felt care, there is no guarantee that that which is so precious to God will not be devalued, diminished to a condition, a commodity. Treated lightly. Treated heavily. Violated. All the mystery, hiddenness gone. All the privacy stripped away. And yet, even in this exposure to others, to leave 'self' lonely.

Who can a person trust? How do they know? They don't really.

Those of us who have suffered abuse, particularly as children, may have very little or no idea as to what might rightfully be expected of life. Taking shame and blame to ourselves for things that were not our fault, maybe trying to gain love and approval from other people, we find ourselves oppressed by the unjust judgments of others. Believing ourselves to be flawed human beings of little or no value, we find our behaviour captive to the demands of our hurting inner selves to be accepted—doing things we don't need to do, in order to achieve impossible ends!

We may limp along, feeling we don't belong, or we don't deserve to belong. Believing that we should be doing better than we are in how we live our lives. But Jesus came to set the captives free, and to lift off the burdens of the oppressed. He came to heal the broken hearted, to rescue and restore his people to life in abundance.

The prophet Zephaniah tells us "Sing aloud, O daughter Zion; shout, O Israel! Rejoice and exult with all your heart O daughter Jerusalem! The LORD has taken away the judgments against you, he has turned away your enemies. The king of Israel, the LORD, is in your midst; you shall fear disaster no more. On that day it shall be said to Jerusalem: Do not fear, O Zion; do not let your hands grow weak. The LORD, your God, is in your midst, a warrior who gives victory; he will rejoice over you with gladness, he will renew you in his love; he will exult over you with loud singing as on a day of festival. I will remove disaster from you, so that you will not bear reproach for it. I will deal with all your oppressors at that time. And I will save the lame and gather the outcast, and I will change their shame into praise and renown in all the earth" (Zeph 3:14–19).

A PROBLEM

We may believe this in our heads, but do we struggle to take it to heart? What difference does it make to re-read this prophecy and put in our own names wherever it says, Jerusalem, or Zion, or Israel? Can we believe it then? It's not necessarily easy to do, if you have been subject to abuse.

Cathy Ann Matthews, in her book Breaking Through writes: "It's strange how, even as a middle-aged woman, I can slip back, so simply, into my childhood needs...It doesn't matter how often I am told I am loved, how often I am shown love and care... Nothing alters my original concepts about myself... no matter how much affirmation others so lovingly give me, my original picture remains unchanged, an intrinsic part of me... I feel unwanted, unlovable, worthless. This heartbreaking knowledge is the reference point on which I have built my whole concept of myself'.[1]

We know that God's Word is truth. We believe it with our minds. But somehow, we fail to be able to take it to heart and live as if it were actually true. Perhaps this is the starting

---

[1] Cathy Ann Matthews, *Breaking Through*, 43, 44.

point—that through reading the truth of God's loving care for us in Scripture, we come to realise we've been believing a lie about ourselves. Having been hard-wired to believe the lies, maybe having never experienced how things were supposed to be, we have no idea what we are supposed to be aiming for.

ARE WE STUCK?

There is therefore no way that we ourselves are going to be able to change our viewpoint of ourselves. We're stuck. The starting point to healing, therefore, is to recognise the 'stuckness.' God knows we can't change ourselves. We need to know that too. We need him to rewire our understanding of how things are supposed to be, and to renew how our minds work. We also need to know what is required of us in this venture.

As we offer this up to God and ask his help, and express our willingness to be changed, he will surely set about doing what he said he would do—set the captives free, relieve the oppressed, heal the broken hearted. He's surely eagerly waiting to help. It's the reason he came on his earthly mission—to deal with sin and all its awful consequences.

So having spent some time considering whether or not we have had right thoughts about God, we now need to consider whether or not we have right thoughts about our own worth. As survivors, what are we to think of ourselves? Was it our fault? Did we deserve this treatment, invite this abuse, secretly desire the shameful things that were done to us? Do we wear some sort of tag which reads 'Pick on me?'

Hiding our wounds becomes a way of life such that we do not even realise we are doing it. These wounds lay buried, unseen and untended, draining our energy and yet covertly governing how we think of ourselves and how we relate to the world. What is it that the world is telling someone who is abused? What is the world telling that person about their worth?

In this second section of studies, we will begin exploring just some of the 'unjust judgments' referred to at the beginning—those that we make over ourselves and those that others make over us—with a view to allowing the Word of God to lead us into freedom. We will consider how the perpetrators of abuse view their victims, and we will consider the power of words to build up and tear down. We will also spend time reviewing the feelings of guilt, shame and blame that are unloaded onto survivors, and the secrecy and loneliness that are the result of trying to hide it all away. But in this journey, where do we start? We start at the beginning, with our name.

I AM PRECIOUS TO GOD?

God speaks to us through the prophet Isaiah, "Do not fear, for I have redeemed you; I have called you by name, you are mine… you are precious in my sight, and honoured, and I love you…" (Is 43:1, 4). We know, intellectually, we are loved and valued by God, because he sent Jesus to rescue us, but are we able to behave as if this were true? How secure is our self-esteem? How confident are we, when faced with the challenges of life? "Precious?" "Honoured?" "Loved?" We may struggle to grasp the truth of this. If we have not experienced unconditional selfless love toward us somewhere in our lives, how are we to know what it is we are missing? It is an alien experience to be required to bear the intense scrutiny of the One who is perfect love.

This is not the love that should actually be interpreted as "I need you." Nor the love that rightfully should be interpreted as "I lust after your body." Both need and lust demonstrate that the one speaking the words is putting themselves first. True love puts the other first. God's love is to be discerned in his self-giving sacrifice in sending his Son to bear the cost of sin that should have been ours to pay. "The good shepherd lays down his life for the sheep" (Jn 10:11).

However, Scripture is also perfectly plain that our value is not to be found in our making up one of a flock of sheep, for it tells us we are precious to God as individuals. For God does not call us to himself a crowd at a time, or even a group at a time. He calls us one by one by one. And he calls us by our name. Jesus, the good shepherd, "calls his own sheep by name and leads them out" (Jn 10:3).

WHAT'S IN A NAME?

What is in a name? Why is it so important that we have a name that is ours? Our name confers on us the dignity of our worth as a member of the human race. Each of us is known and loved by God, who sent out each life-giving spirit from his own heart to engender that life in us. We are each identified not by numbers and codes as in a vast warehouse from where items are dispatched, but by our name. We are told, in the Old Testament, that our names are engraved on the palms of God's hands (Is 49:16). Were they etched there by the nails of crucifixion?

The power of a name to confer personal identity on an individual is such that a perpetrator will usually never use it before a violent abusive act. Instead, the victim will be designated by any number of derogatory labels, or curses. Instead of seeing the person they are about to assault, the perpetrator sees an object—"You ##!!**." If you have been abused, you can no doubt fill in the gaps with any number of racist, sexist, demeaning and hateful tags. This objectification of a victim is not pre-thought. It is an outworking of the fact that the abuser does not see his or her victim as a person but as an object, a thing devoid of humanity.

I HAVE A NAME! PLEASE USE IT!

During a television programme which was documenting the stories of a number of men who were attempting to overcome their violent behaviour within their homes, one man was asked by the facilitator, "Who was affected by your actions?" The man listed a number of people which included the police, the paramedics, himself, his neighbours. "What about your wife?" he was asked. In response to this question the man looked puzzled. His wife was simply not present on his radar as a person for consideration because, of course, he had been seeing her only as an object.

Pamela Cooper-White, a pastor with vast experience of helping victims of abuse, makes the comprehensive assertion that "labelling or name-calling (spoken or unspoken), happens before every violent act in our world."[2] However, this objectification of the victim can and does occur in all social contexts not just in a violent assault. Many of you will know that it occurs in the home, at school, at work, out shopping, even in church. It can be connected to what you look like, what you choose to wear, your race, your gender, your religion. It is vast in scope and can be devastating in impact.

Objectification can be blatant but unspoken. Pornography is a hidden, rotten core in society, portraying its dehumanising,

---

2   Pamela Cooper-White, *The Cry of Tamar*, 20.

demeaning message wordlessly not only in every newsagent in Australia, but also potentially every computer connected to the internet. The men, women and children portrayed in such films are objects to be ogled and lusted after. Is their full birth name listed in the credits of the video in which they appeared?

But objectification can also be quite subtle. So subtle in fact that no label may be given at all. One woman tells of how her father—who had abused her throughout her childhood—thanked her husband by name, "and your dear wife" for the outing that they had arranged that day. The woman herself was standing there with them. It was apparently quite usual for him to speak this way, not acknowledging her presence at all, or even looking at her. This was, therefore, not just a playful use of language but was borne of the mindset of not ever seeing his daughter as a person in her own right.

However God, our heavenly father, demonstrating his loving concern for and knowledge of his children, with singular focus, calls each one of us using our name. Thus, according to us the dignity of our humanity and affirming to us the immense value of our unique self. This is where we start in our consideration of our thoughts about ourselves.

QUESTIONS

1. Since the beginning of time, God has granted men and women the privilege of naming not only the creatures, but also each other, and especially their children. In each case there is usually a reason given for the name.

   - Read Genesis 3:20; 4:25; 29:32–35; 35:18; and 1 Samuel 1:20.

   a) Do you like your birth name? Have you changed it in any way? If so, why?

   b) What do your own personal names mean? (Excluding your family name).

   c) Do you know the reason why you were given those particular names?

   d) Were you named after a relative, and if so, are you happy about it? Why or why not?

2. God says we are of immense value to him.

   - Read Psalm 139:1–4, 13–18; Isaiah 43:3–7; 49:15–16; and John 3:16–17.

   a) Psalm 139 tells us that God knows us inside out. How does he know that?

   b) What does it mean to you to know that you are fearfully and wonderfully made?

c) Just as God loved Israel, so he loves us. Do you agree that you are precious to God, and honoured by him, and loved by him. Why or why not?

d) How you manage your own health can sometimes indicate the extent to which you value yourself. Do you take good care of yourself? Why or why not?

e) To what lengths has God gone to demonstrate His love for us?

3. Scripture tells us the detailed story of how the boy Samuel was called into relationship with God.
    - Read 1 Samuel 3:1–10; and Isaiah 43:1.

    a) Did Samuel know God before this event? Does this surprise you?

    b) There are possibly variations to your name, or you may answer to a family nickname. Which name does God call you by?

    c) What does it mean to you to know that God himself, calls you by name?

    d) Samuel knew from the start that he was to be a prophet. What do you think God is, or will be entrusting you with, as your ministry?

4. Within the overarching story of David's reign as King of Israel there is the story of the rape of his daughter, Tamar, by one of her half-brothers, Amnon. They are both David's children, by different mothers.
    - Read 2 Samuel 13:1–22.

a) The narrator of the story says Amnon 'loved' Tamar. Would you call it love? Why or why not?

b) How does Amnon refer to Tamar before he rapes her? (v11). And after the rape? (v17).

c) What were Tamar's feelings after the event?

d) Do you understand this principle of objectification and does it resonate with you or someone you know?

e) Tamar was not only violated by Amnon, but also by her brother, Absalom, because he told her to keep quiet about it, and not take it to heart. And by her father who did nothing for her. The details of this assault are not necessary to the overall story of David's reign. Why do you think God might have included it in the Bible?

5. God calls us by name, and as we trust in him, he gives us his family name, Christian. As a result of this our names are recorded in the book of life in heaven.

- Read Jeremiah 15:16; John 10:3–6; Philippians 4:3; Hebrews 12:22–23; Revelation 20:11–15; and 22:4.

a) The disciples did not understand what Jesus was talking about when he spoke of his sheep recognising his voice as they heard their names called. Do you?

b) Jeremiah said that he was called by God's name. And in Revelation 22:4 it tells us that God's name is written on our foreheads. This means that if we have put our trust in Jesus, we bear his name, as well as our own. What might this mean to you?

c) It seems that a record of the lives of each of us on earth is kept in heaven, under our own, individual name. What are your thoughts concerning this?

d) Is your name written in the book of life? If not, would you like it to be? (If so, this is a free gift of God. See Jn 5:24; 6:40, and Rom 6:23)

STUDY 7: STICKS AND STONES

> "In the beginning God created the heavens and the earth. The earth was empty, a formless mass cloaked in darkness. And the Spirit of God was hovering over its surface. And God said, 'Let there be light,' and there was light..." (Gen 1:1-3 NLT).

Such was the power of the spoken word of God that it brought the universe into being! God spoke "and so it was;" and when he had finished, his creation was "excellent in every way."

On the final day of creation, the sixth day, God had said "Let us make people in our image, to be like ourselves...So God created people in his own image; God patterned them after himself; male and female he created them" (Gen 1:26–27 NLT). And then he blessed them—the first blessing pronounced in Scripture.

What were humankind being blessed with? There are two critically important 'gifts' with which we were blessed, which belong only to those made in the image of God. Both bring with them almost terrifying responsibility. One was free will, which we discussed in Study 3 God's Sovereignty. This gift means that we can make choices including what we choose to believe, and what we choose to do. We therefore can choose to believe God or not, and we can choose to say 'Yes' or 'No' to God. No other created being has been entrusted with this responsibility.

The other key blessing is the ability to exchange thoughts with each other through words—we were given language. Why is this such a daunting responsibility? It is because there is power in the use of words. Scripture tells us God's spoken words have the power to bring the universe into being. As we are made in God's image, our words have power too. Not power to bring a universe into being, but power sufficient to speak life or death into someone's life. We are warned in the book of Proverbs "Death and life are in the power of the tongue, and those who love it will eat its fruit" (18:21). Power indeed! Such is the potential of this gift that we are told that we may be required to give account for every careless word we have spoken when we come to judgment! Speaking to the Pharisees, Jesus said "I tell you, on the day of judgment you will have to give an account for every careless word you utter, for by your words you will be justified, and by your words you will be condemned" (Mt 12:36–37).

WE CAN CHOOSE!

What do we do with these amazing gifts of free will and speech? Do we choose to believe what God says, and do we choose to use our own words wisely? It would be wonderful if we always chose to speak out good and encouraging words, because language used in this way has life-giving power. But Scripture, and experience, tell us that our tongues are not easily tamed. We are warned that one minute we praise God, and in the very next breath we curse others who are made in the image of God (Js 3:9). It seems we can so easily choose to speak death into someone's life.

More to the point in this series of studies, what words have others chosen to speak over us? Were they life-giving or death-delivering? And have we chosen to believe them and to act as if they were true—chosen to take them to heart? If so, those words have come to control our behaviour. Just as importantly, what words have we chosen to speak over ourselves? And have we believed them? Have we spoken truth or lie, life or death into our own lives?

OUR WOUNDS

There is not one of us who has not been hurt by the words of others. A common playground chant when I was a child was "Sticks and stones may break my bones, but words will never hurt me." But this is just not true, words can hurt us, and do great injury.

In the previous study we considered the words used to objectify individual victims, particularly before a violent attack. However, demeaning words are used in everyday situations, at home, at work, at school, or even just in ordinary daily transactions. You will find yourself on the receiving end of these words if you are judged to be not the right age, or gender, or size, or race, or social status, or even if you don't wear the right clothes or have the right hair style.

And the power of these words is indisputable. My husband and I owned and ran a coffee shop for some years. And such is the ability of relatively mild abusive words that, even as a mature adult, it would take me two or three days to recover my composure from the attitude and words of just one abusive customer. This is not physical assault, yet the wounds are very real, and may take time to heal.

The Apostle Paul tells us that words can act like flaming

darts or fiery arrows (Eph 6:16). They stick into your psyche and can smoulder away, eroding your self-confidence sometimes for a lifetime. One elderly lady I had the privilege to call friend incurred just such a wound. When a girl on the brink of womanhood, her father had likened her nose to a 'cherry picker', meaning she had a hooked nose. I hadn't noticed anything out of the ordinary with her nose myself, but these words had stuck in her mind, eroding her self-confidence for her entire life, for they were still being repeated by her when she was well into her eighties.

TAKING IT TO HEART

It is encouraging to know that we have a choice between believing what is spoken over us, or not. In order to be able to do this, it is important to be able to distinguish the difference between firstly, understanding what is said; secondly, believing whether it to be true or not; and thirdly, taking it to heart. For example, we may understand that someone thinks we are an idiot. But do we choose to agree with them? Do we believe it? Perhaps we have even called ourselves an idiot. If we allow this thought to stand, unchallenged in our own thinking, it becomes the value we place on ourselves. We have taken it to heart.

How we value ourselves is of immense importance because whether we notice it or not, it determines our behaviour. We may unconsciously spend a lifetime trying to prove the person wrong, who spoke these words over us. Or maybe we try to prove to ourselves that they were wrong. On the other hand, we may spend a lifetime not trying at all, because we are, after all, just an idiot. This is, of course, contrary to what God says about us. So we are, in fact, telling God he got it wrong!

THE DEEPEST CUTS

The words that have power to cut the deepest are spoken over us by those we want to please, and the younger we are, the greater the potential damage. And so it is that parents and teachers wield great power concerning the words they speak over their children and pupils. As children we are learning how we shape up in the world. 'Have I got what it takes?' 'Am I loved?' 'Am I worthy of being loved?' 'Do I fit in?' 'Is it OK to be good at something?' Basically, we are seeking to discover if we qualify as a worth-while human being.

As we attempt to discover who we are, we process the feedback from those nearest to us. What are they telling us? And if the feedback is all negative, do we simply believe what we are told about ourselves? What have we taken to heart? The result can be gaping wounds in soul and spirit that we may not even recognise are there, but which nevertheless control how we move forward in life.

As adults we have more life experience to draw on, and have the ability to assess our situation more objectively. But a child believes what he or she is told. The responsibility of adults to take care what words they choose to speak over youngsters is immense. 'You will never amount to any good' may actually become reality for the child. The power of the words act as a curse. 'Here comes the trouble-maker' has the potential to speak such an outcome into existence.

WHAT WE LONG FOR

When we are only given negative feedback, we long for positive affirmation. Cathy Ann Matthews expresses feelings that are common to many survivors of childhood abuse—a sometimes insatiable appetite for affirmation. She writes: "I used to have an almost insatiable need for approval. It is one of the most difficult indicators for survivors to live with. Without being aware of it, I used many unconscious and even conscious ploys and manipulations to get someone to meet that need… Such a tremendous need to be loved and accepted!…Though I did not realise it, I was really filled with longing for my parents to love and accept me…My parents, deep down, did not accept me or love me. They did not even want me…"[1]

The words of affirmation we desire so much are never forthcoming, and we curse ourselves as dumb and stupid. We tell ourselves 'I will never be able to do this' and 'I am obviously not good enough.' Even more than this, we may vow such things as never to make ourselves vulnerable to such pain again. In doing so, we bind ourselves in chains of our own making. For as the words of these vows start to exert their power, we find a wall has gone up, and we are having difficulty in relating to people with whom we would like to be close.

THE TRUTH WILL SET YOU FREE

What remedy is there for having believed the negative words that have been spoken over us? Or for never having had any positive words spoken into our lives? Where can we turn to when our most basic emotional needs are not met, and never can be met by those who should have expressed love for us?

It is a tragedy that abuse can drive a survivor away from the one being who can and will tell them the truth about themselves. Cathy Ann Matthews came to understand that

---

1   Cathy Ann Matthews *Breaking Through*, 176–177.

her need for positive affirmation would not ever be met by her earthly parents. Fortunately, she turned to God for her answers, and so did I. As I have mentioned previously, very early in my Christian journey and a long time before I started on the more recent intensive healing of my hidden wounds, I discovered in Psalm 139:13 that I had originated from the heart of God. It was a great revelation to me that I was his child first and foremost, and that he had entrusted me to my earthly parents for them to raise me. It made a huge difference to how I felt about myself. I could now ask myself 'What does God have to say about me? Other people's opinions of us may vary, but Scripture informs us of our true value.

WHAT DOES GOD THINK ABOUT ME?

The whole of Scripture tells us how much God wants to have relationship with us, because he loves us. But we find the Apostle Paul, in his letter to the Ephesians, almost tripping over his own words as he attempts to communicate to us all that God wants to bless us with. He begins the letter with a long list of these spiritual blessings that Christians can take as truth about themselves. They include being loved, chosen, adopted into God's family, and being counted holy and blameless before God. We are told we are redeemed, forgiven, and lavished with grace. We now have a purpose in life and an inheritance to be enjoyed in a future we can look forward to. God has even given us his Holy Spirit to live within us. And amazingly, God delights to bless us with all these things (Eph 1:3–14).

Armed with this truth, we can begin to recognise the lies that have been spoken over us, or that we have spoken over ourselves. We can then decide whether we are going to believe the lies, or believe God's truth concerning ourselves.

CAN WE BELIEVE IT?

In our own strength we will find it impossible to defuse the power of negative words that we have taken to heart. They keep on ringing in our ears no matter how hard we try to silence them. But it is God himself who will extinguish the fiery darts as we offer up our wounds to him for healing. We know that people involved in competitive sports are taught psychological techniques that enable them to believe in themselves and their abilities, and to visualise victory. But if our own words have power to bring about positive outcomes in our lives, how much more is the power of God's word able to work for good within us?

Believing what God has had written in Scripture for us is therefore far more than a psychological exercise—it is a spiritual exercise. For the Word of God is "living and active" (Heb 4:12). Though we may struggle to believe these truths in our own strength, nevertheless, as we read and reread the truths of Scripture concerning ourselves, the power of God will go to work transforming our thinking and strengthening our faith. And our faith is grounded in the finished work of Christ on the cross, on our behalf.

CURSE AND BLESSING

In the foreword to her husband's book, *Blessing or Curse: You can choose*, Ruth Prince tells how, before they were married, she had asked him to pray concerning her legs, for they were hurting her so much. But surprisingly, instead of simply praying for healing, he prayed positivity and thanks over them! He then explained to her that he had been 'unsaying' something that Ruth may have spoken over her legs many years before. And the pain went away. She then remembered that as a teenager she had said she hated her legs![2]

In explaining how blessings and curses operate, Derek Prince states that the main vehicle for both of them is words. Words that are spoken or written or merely uttered inwardly. He explains, "Both blessings and curses belong to the invisible, spiritual realm. They are vehicles of supernatural, spiritual power. Blessings produce good and beneficial results; curses produce bad and harmful results. Both are major themes of Scripture."[3]

We thank God for encouraging words that have been spoken over us, and specific blessings that have been pronounced to our benefit. We find it impossible to completely discount the effects of curses that we know have been directed our way just by trying in our own strength. But in Jesus we have been provided with a way out from under these curses, to take hold of the blessings God wants to release into our lives.

For Jesus not only took on himself the weight of all of our sin when he was crucified. He also took on himself all of the curses that were spoken against us by others, and all the curses that we have spoken over ourselves. "…it is written: 'Cursed is everyone who hangs on a tree'—in order that in Christ Jesus the blessing of Abraham might come to the Gentiles, so that we might receive the promise of the Spirit through faith" (Gal 3:13–14). Jesus is therefore able and willing to absorb into his

---

[2] Derek Prince, *Blessing and Curse, You can choose*, 9–10.

[3] Derek Prince, *Blessing and Curse*, 33.

own self all the curses spoken into our lives, if we yield them up to him for remedy.

Jesus is the Word of God. And the word is truth. As we choose to read Scripture, and believe it, and act on it, these words will become secured in our understanding of ourselves and God—they will dwell in us. Unlike the lies spoken over us which were destroying us, this truth will bring life and blessing. Hopefully, as we choose to move into freedom, we will also choose to use the power of our own words to speak truth and life into the lives of others.

QUESTIONS

1. Words carry great power, both for good and evil, life and death.

    - Read Genesis 31:30–35; 35:16–21; Proverbs 18:21; Matthew 12:36–37; Ephesians 6:16–17; and James 3:7–10.

    a) The New Living Translation version of Proverbs 18:21 reads, "Those who love to talk will experience the consequences, for the tongue can kill or nourish life." Share any thoughts that come to mind when reading this verse.

    b) Jacob did not know that he was cursing his wife when he spoke concerning his father-in-law's gods (Gen 31:32). What happened anyway?

    c) Can you identify any flaming arrows with which you were showered—words that have stuck in your memory, causing you pain? If so, how have you dealt with the burning pain? If at all.

    d) How does Paul say we are to deal with the flaming arrows? How do we exercise faith?

2. Our own words carry power, but the power of God's words is immeasurably greater. We exercise faith by taking God at his word and speaking out this truth. In this way, the

Word of God can be used like a sword, cutting through lies we may have taken to heart.

- Read John 1:1; 5:24; 15:3; 17:17; Thessalonians 2:13; 2 Timothy 3:14–16; and Hebrews 1:3; 4:12.

    a) What evidence do you find in these verses that God's word brings life?

    b) Which verses tell us that God's word itself is alive? What do you understand by this?

    c) What are some of the things that God's word is accomplishing in a believer's life?

    d) 1 Thessalonians 2:13 tells us that God's word is at work within a believer. What do you think God's word is accomplishing in your life?

3. We learn our value in community by the words people speak over us. In this OT story, we see a young woman caught up in a drama where her conniving father uses her to manipulate the man who actually loves her younger sister. She longs for affirmation that she is loved.

    - Read Genesis 29:15–35; and 31:14–15.

    a) What were Laban's daughters apparently worth to him?

    b) What do you think Leah's feelings are concerning herself, and the unfolding drama in which she is required to participate.

    c) Note what Leah said on each occasion that she bore a son. What was Leah hoping for?

- d) To whom did she finally look, after the birth of her fourth son?

- e) Does any part of this story resonate with any part of your own life?

4. The power of words spoken over us, either by others or by ourselves, can act as a curse. We can curse ourselves and come under a curse from other people.

   - Read Genesis 27:1–14, 30–38; Matthew 27:24–26; Deuteronomy 21:22–23; Galatians 3:13–14; and Proverbs 26:2.

   - a) From the story in Genesis 27, how seriously did the family believe the power of the spoken word, blessings and curses to be? Could the words be unsaid?

   - b) If Jesus has become a curse for us, what happens to the curses spoken over our lives if we commit them to Jesus?

   - c) How do you think you will go about defusing the power of negative words over your life?

   - d) In Christ we are made right with God. Because of this, we do not provide any foothold for a curse to alight on us as it would be underserved or unfair. How can you use the truth of Proverbs 26:2 to good effect into the future?

5. God's desire is to be able to shower us with blessing.

   - Read Deuteronomy 30:19–20; Matthew 5:1–12; Ephesians 1:3–14; and Romans 12:2.

a) In the Deuteronomy reading, which choice would you say you have made?

b) Which do you think holds more power—a curse spoken out over you, or a blessing spoken out over you. Why?

c) From Jesus' teaching, what are some of the blessings that will come to those who trust in him.

The power of God's Word to make a difference in our lives is awesome. We may have been controlled for decades by lies spoken over us and it will take time and effort on our part to allow our minds to be re-programmed so that we are able to embrace blessing.

Some survivors who struggle with believing God's opinion of them have printed out positive verses and stuck them on the fridge, on the bathroom mirror or above their desk so that they can be reminded of God's truth about themselves daily.

d) How can you set things up so that God's word can dwell in you, constantly working to bring life and healing into your life?

Completing the table on the following page may be helpful.

SINNED AGAINST

Some of the blessings that we are promised in Christ Jesus in Ephesians 1:3–14 have been listed in the table below. Check out the list and record where you are at with each blessing. Ask God to help you take to heart these blessings, so they help you move forward in life.

Verse	Blessing	Understand	Believe	Embraced
2	Grace and peace			
3	Within Christ			
3	Blessed with every spiritual blessing			
4, 11	Chosen			
4	Holy and blameless			
4	Abundantly loved			
5	Adopted, child of God			
5	Bringing joy to God			
7	Redeemed			
7	Forgiven			
8	Grace poured out over us			
9	Enlightened			
11	Within God's purpose			
12, 14	Bringing God praise and glory			
13	Marked/sealed with the Holy Spirit			
11, 14	Guaranteed inheritance			

STUDY 8: SHAME ON YOU!

To be treated as an object, rather than a person, is to feel a burden in your soul. The heaviness of rejection is immense. Likewise, the power of curses in our lives can do their hidden work, dragging us into defeat and despair. It is a wonder, sometimes, that survivors can walk upright, carrying so much weight of negativity. Shortly after I had chosen to entrust my life to Jesus, a woman from the village where I lived told me I walked differently. More confidently! She knew nothing whatsoever about me, except that I lived locally. What difference will it make in our lives as we continue to explore what Jesus has done for us, take hold of these truths, and walk into more and more freedom?

Genesis 1, the beginning of the whole story of the truth concerning the relationship between God and humankind, is where we started our previous study. It may be no surprise that in this following study we still find ourselves in the first chapters of Genesis, as we continue our exploration of our "very good" beginnings and how it all went very wrong. It is here, in the unfolding story of Adam and Eve, that we recognise with startling clarity the dynamics of relationship that have remained unchanged down through the millennia, and which are still causing us such misery today.

A potent mix of deception, guilt, shame, blame, and secrecy

is blended together as paradise unravels. The disobedience of Adam and Eve exposed them to the judgment of God, so they tried to hide their guilt. In their exposure, they also realised they were naked and sought to cover their shame. As judgment was about to fall, they attempted to pass the blame. Absolutely nothing has changed!

The guilt and shame that Adam and Eve felt were rightfully theirs to bear. And they are rightfully ours to feel, if we have truly been guilty of disobeying God. In feeling these emotions, we are given opportunity to recognise our errors and make amends. We can turn to God and say sorry and ask for forgiveness. And by God's grace, ministered to us through Jesus Christ, we can have things put right. But as survivors of abuse, is all the guilt and shame we may feel, rightly ours to bear?

In this fallen, twisted world not everyone wants to take note of feelings of guilt and shame, and heed their warning. Instead they do as Adam and Eve did. And if their offence is against others, they attempt to stick that guilt and the shame onto their victim. Where it doesn't belong.

However, this is not all that the victim is made to wear as a result of the abuse, because the perpetrators seek relief from their own uncomfortable feelings of shame by blaming the victim for what, in fact, were their own actions. Added to this, if shifting the blame does not quite work, they may coerce their victim in any number of ways, depending on the circumstances, to keep silent about what happened. We will consider the actions of deception, blaming and secrecy in Study 9 and 10. But here in this study, we will focus on the feelings of guilt and shame.

Where a victim is made to feel these emotions on account of

what was done to them, how is the survivor to cope with this grossly unfair situation? What relief can he or she manufacture, because for the survivor, it is not a guilty action which initiates the feelings. Instead, shaming occurs first and hot on its heels come feelings of guilt. Maybe put there by the perpetrator through blaming, maybe through the survivor's own self-doubt. Possibly both. 'Was it my fault?' Thus a complex web of emotions entangles sinner and sinned against. How is it possible to be extricated from this situation into a place of victory over the abuse? What are emotions anyway? Where do they come from and why?

THE ORIGIN OF EMOTIONS

Scripture reveals to us time and again that God expresses feelings. He feels joy and grief, anger and delight, love and hate.[1] And as we are made in the image of God, we express these feelings too. However, there are two key differences between how we experience emotions and how God experiences emotions. These differences arise because nothing ever takes God by surprise, and he is always fully in control of himself. Therefore, emotions do not just arrive and affect him unannounced, as they do with us. This means he can choose to experience them. And he is never swept along, out of control on a strong tide of feelings, as sometimes might happen with ourselves.

It should be a wonder to us that God would choose to experience some of the emotions, because so often, it seems, they are uncomfortable. Why, for example, would anyone choose to feel grief or unrequited love? Millions of people find

---

1 Gen 6:6; Is 54:8; Is 62:5; Jer 31:20; Amos 5:21; and Zeph 3:17.

some feelings so painful they seek to dull them with alcohol or drugs, or by watching too much television or by disappearing into a book or onto the internet.

Coming seemingly out of nowhere, loneliness, anger, sadness, anxiety and fear arrive uninvited and can hang around indefinitely if not dealt with. They can overwhelm us and cause us to do things we may later regret. Indeed, sometimes we cannot manage them ourselves without professional help, and possibly medication. Why has God given them to us, particularly the uncomfortable ones? Careful thought reveals that originally this endless variety of emotions were, and still are in fact, gifts and it is not difficult to understand why.

HOW DO THEY HELP US?

If we look once again at what is happening with Adam and Eve, we can see that one of the functions of emotions is to tell us what is happening in our relationships with each other and with God. They therefore inform us as to how we are tracking through life. As with Adam and Eve, the feelings prompt us to recognise our circumstances, and we can then make a choice as to how we will respond. So, just as we can physically feel the heat of a fire, and therefore decide to keep away from it to avoid being burnt, so also we can feel anxiety, or fear, in response to any situation we find ourselves in. If it feels scary to walk down a dark alleyway on our own, we can choose not to. If we felt no fear, we may walk into danger.

These emotions can cause us to do things like make friends, say sorry, get married, throw a party, or seek safety. They can also prompt road rage, assault, and unkind words. If we are alert to their message, however, we can ask 'Why am I feeling guilty, depressed, angry, in love, happy, sad?' and so on. And we can consciously choose what to do about it or ask for help if need be.

So often, however, we do not notice what we are feeling, and fail to make an appropriate response. Unfortunately for Adam and Eve, they chose to hide from God rather than run to him and say sorry. Who knows what the outcome might have been for us if they had made a different choice?

COMING, READY OR NOT

It came as a surprise to me to recognise that we can't manufacture emotions. Joy and grief arise inevitably, in response to life. And because we can't stop them coming, there is no reason for us to feel guilty about having a feeling, or not having a feeling. We cannot make ourselves feel love for someone, nor can we stop ourselves feeling sad. We can, however, choose how to react to them. For example, say we feel furious. Why? Because that person jumped the queue in front of us. Driven along by our anger do we bowl up to them and give them a piece of our mind? Maybe we haven't the courage to do that, so we boil inwardly, seething in rage and impotence. Or perhaps, recognising the source of our anger we choose to let it go, so that it doesn't continue to bother us.

So having recognised our feelings, and their context, we can then choose to address the negative ones—"Do not let your hearts be troubled, and do not let them be afraid" (Jn 14:27)—perhaps by standing on a relevant God-given promise, or maybe by seeking the wise help of others. And we can choose to embrace the positive feelings and enjoy them—"You have turned my mourning into dancing; you have taken off my sackcloth and clothed me with joy" (Ps 30:11).

STRATEGY FOR A SURVIVOR

Making things more complicated for a survivor of abuse is the fact that emotions rarely seem to arrive neatly in recognisable singularity. Instead, there are often several feelings mixed up together, making it difficult to sort out what's what. But understanding the difference can be important. As we have found with Adam and Eve, shame can be felt with guilt, but these are often confused in a survivor's understanding. How do we distinguish between them?

Lewis B. Smedes, in his book Shame and Grace, points out that guilt relates to what we do, but shame relates to who we are. He says: "The feeling of shame is about our very selves, not about some bad thing we did or said, but about who we are. A person may feel guilty for telling a lie to his wife and feel shame for being the sort of person who would do such a thing."[2]

So guilt concerns something specific we may have done, or not done. It can therefore be relatively easy to discern what is making us feel guilty. And whether we should rightfully be feeling guilty, or not, in an abusive situation in which we have found ourselves, depends on who is blaming whom. Either the perpetrator is blaming us, or we are blaming ourselves. We will tackle this issue in Study 9.

However, shame concerns our very selves. Who we are. Or who we think we are. Smedes explains "… shame is a very heavy feeling. It is a feeling that we do not measure up and maybe never will measure up to the sorts of persons we are meant to be. The feeling, when we are conscious of it, gives us

---

[2] Lewis B. Smedes, *Shame and Grace: Healing the shame we don't deserve*, 9.

a vague disgust with ourselves, which in turn feels like a hunk of lead on our hearts."[3]

Shame is like a sticky dough or glue. It seems to stick to everything within reach. And sexual abuse elicits the most profound shame for the victim. For it is the very soul of the person—their hidden self—that is exposed and violated. As a new Christian, I remember feeling embarrassed to hear a missionary telling her story of how she was held captive and raped during an uprising in the country where she was working. I thought "How could she share such a shameful thing—and in a public meeting!" She had already processed the rights and wrongs of this event, but as a hearer of her ordeal, I was feeling her undeserved shame, which in my imagination must still be stuck to her. Now it seemed it was also stuck to me!

Whatever the cause of our shame, because it is about our sense of self, we are most vulnerable to experiencing it when we feel ourselves exposed and are found to be wanting. As we have discussed in Study 7, a survivor of abuse will have been treated as an object, less than human, and so feelings of shame are an inevitable outcome.

The shame arises therefore, because the victim is exposed in a situation in which they are unable to adequately defend themselves. It may occur in public, such as bullying, or in the privacy of a bedroom. It can occur in daylight or in dead of night. The exposure may be physical—an actual nakedness, such as may occur in sexual assault. Or it may be one of a thousand supposed weaknesses held up for ridicule to serve as an ongoing source of entertainment for the abuser(s).

---

[3] Lewis B. Smedes, *Shame and Grace*, 5.

IT'S NOT FAIR!

Shame, as we have seen, can of course be a good thing if we really are less than we are meant to be. If we are guilty of something, for which we are ashamed, we can make amends, say sorry, try to put things right. However, the fact that abusers often stick their shame onto their victim means that we need to discern whether what we are feeling is actually ours to wear. Have we become ashamed because we have been forced into participating in an act that we think is shameful? Did we have any power to prevent that? Or have we unwittingly taken the offenders' shame onto ourselves, because we think that for some reason or other we deserved it, or brought it on ourselves on account of something we did, or didn't do.

Pamela Cooper-White, in talking about women who are subject to domestic violence states: "To leave [the relationship] is to admit defeat, and this defeat is in the area in which women are most expected to excel—the area of relationships and care. It is ironic and tragic that a person who is beaten by an intimate partner will feel ashamed, but that same person would not hesitate to report or discuss being held up by a stranger on the street."[4]

If we don't have a secure idea of our own worth, we may be more vulnerable to taking undeserved shame to heart. It is a burden that is not ours to carry. As survivors, we need to be able to recognise the difference between deserved and undeserved shame so that we can deal with it effectively.

---

[4] Pamela Cooper-White, *The Cry of Tamar*, 116.

HEALING

There are psychological techniques that may help survivors in their struggles, but fortunately, as Christians, we do not have to rely only on these for healing. God has not missed seeing any of the details of our lives, whether we have tried to hide them or not. As we look to him for discernment, he shines the light of truth into the deception of unfair, undeserved feelings. He breaks their chains by his Word, setting us at liberty to discover and enjoy our true selves.

As we his children call out to him for refuge from our exposure, Christ covers us with his robes of righteousness. We can then move into victory over offensive deceptions by refusing, in Jesus' name, to accept them. We can speak out the truth of Scripture, which informs us of our own worth before God, and we can look to him for our vindication.

Jesus took on himself our guilt on the cross, so that we might be considered guilt-free before God. But perhaps most startlingly, Jesus submitted himself to being exposed, completely naked for all the world to see, at his crucifixion. In the undeserved shame of that event, Jesus took upon himself all our shame. The comfort that this speaks to survivors, who have themselves been exposed, physically or otherwise, is immeasurable. That Jesus would allow that to happen, and so fully identify with our suffering speaks of his great and tender love for each one of us.

A profoundly touching example of this love was given me some years ago when I used to help a severely disabled teenage girl with her lunch every Friday. She had cerebral palsy and was unable to walk or speak. When I arrived one day, it was to find her with head down. Very depressed. The staff told me she had been sexually interfered with. How they had discovered this I do not know.

During our private time at lunch I spoke to her of Jesus, as I was pretty sure she already had relationship with him. I then prayed that he would wash her clean from all the shame. Top to toe. After prayer, she lifted her head and was radiant! She went back into school waving her arms in glee! The staff were amazed. I wasn't supposed to share 'religion' at school, and because she couldn't speak I thought I would be in the clear. However, when they asked her how the change had come about, she clasped her hands together in the unmistakeable gesture of prayer. So, thankfully, God got the glory after all.

⋯ QUESTIONS

1. The undeserved shame we feel as a result of abuse often arises in public. Others, besides our abuser, view our supposed weakness, or inability to defend ourselves.
   - Read John 8:2–11; and Leviticus 20:10.

   a) This woman was, in fact, guilty of adultery. She should be feeling deserved guilt and shame for her sin before God. However, the situation she then finds herself in is even more shaming. Is this second shaming deserved or underserved? Why?

   b) Picture the scene. What mix of emotions do you think she would be feeling at this time? Does any part of this scenario resonate with your experience?

   c) The law states that the man should come under judgment too. But he is not there. What are your thoughts on this?

   d) Jesus dealt with all the accusers with one simple sentence, turning the tables on them and exposing their own shortcomings. What would you like Jesus to say to those who have abused you?

   e) Do you think the woman sinned in this way again? Why or why not?

2. To be naked is to have nothing hidden from view. All is exposed.
   - Read Genesis 2:24–25; 3:7–11; John 3:19–21; Revelation 3:18; and 16:15.

   a) Why do you think it was that Adam and Eve were naked "and they were not ashamed?"

   b) In the reading from John's Gospel, why do you think people still love darkness rather than light? What are they trying to hide?

   c) In Scripture, nakedness seems to be accompanied by shame. What are your thoughts on this?

   d) In Genesis 3:7a, we find that Adam and Eve both have their eyes "opened" and they "knew" that they were naked. In other words, they now felt shame. Is this shame deserved? Why or why not?

   e) What do Adam and Eve choose to do in response to this changed situation? What else could they have chosen to do?

3. When shamed, we desperately feel the need to be covered, or hidden, or clothed.
   - Read Genesis 3:21; Psalm 91:1–4; Isaiah 61:10; Matthew 23:37; Galatians 3:27; and Hebrews 4:13.

   a) What clothing has God provided for you through Christ? What do you understand by this?

   b) There are a number of different images given in these verses that describe how we can be covered or protected by God. Which is your favourite and why?

c) Why do you think God would want to cover you?

d) Do you mind having your every thought, word and deed always on full view to God? Why or why not?

4. Jesus himself was profoundly shamed when exposed to public ridicule at his crucifixion.

- Read Genesis 9:20–23; Exodus 20:26; Nahum 3:5; Matthew 27:27–44; and Hebrews 12:2.

a) In the Matthew reading, in what different ways was Jesus shamed? Was this shame deserved or undeserved? Why do you think he endured it? (What was he looking forward to?)

b) There are cultural differences as regards modesty and clothing. The OT readings give some idea of Jewish culture, and God's expectations concerning nakedness. How shameful do you think it would have been for Jesus, his family and the disciples, for him to be crucified naked?

c) A depiction of the crucifixion rarely represents Jesus totally naked. Why do you think this is?

d) What do you think Jesus' nakedness in such a situation might mean to someone who has been stripped and violated, whether publicly or not?

5. Feelings of undeserved shame are stuck on us by our abusers. But God undertakes to bring light and justice into our situations.

- Read Psalm 6:8–10; 25:1–3; 135:13–14; Isaiah 54:4–5, 17; Romans 9:33; and 1 Corinthians 1:26–31.

a) Time and again, throughout the Psalms we hear the plea "Don't let me be put to shame." What does God promise concerning shame and a believer? What does this mean to you?

b) In the letter to the Corinthians, which type of people does God have in mind to put to shame? Why do you think this is?

c) What does God promise concerning your vindication? Are you looking forward to this?

d) What does God promise concerning those who have abused you, if they do not repent?

e) Which promise means the most to you. And why?

STUDY 9: WHO'S TO BLAME?

> 'It wasn't my fault! It was hers! And you gave her to me!' says Adam. 'No, no. It wasn't my fault. The serpent deceived me!' says Eve. And so, we find the dynamics of blame and being deceived at the heart of all the troubles that have beset humankind since creation (Gen.3:12-13).

The interplay between the four characters taking part in this drama, God, Adam, Eve and the serpent have set the template for our inter-relationships ever since. However, we have difficulty in discussing what is happening here with any measure of useful objectivity because one of the chief characters is a man, and another, a woman.

Have you ever been in a mixed-gender Bible study group when the issue of the original sin has come up? A certain tension arises as we steel ourselves to cope with divergent opinions as to who was to blame. The difficulty is that we tend to identify strongly with our own gender, which renders rational discussion almost impossible. We can't seem to help it. I am on Eve's side of course, my husband on Adam's. It takes much grace to navigate the tension and secure the truth of the matter without someone taking offence! How can I, a woman, possibly promote discussion on this matter entirely impartially? The same would apply, of course, if I were a man.

We must do our best to look to Scripture for our answers, and to God for grace to consider the situation rationally. For this event has unconsciously been foundational to shaping the mindset of how men and women interrelate even to this day. And so it is still causing much grief. How this works out in relationships between man and woman, husband and wife will be explored in more depth in Study 13, where we explore the marriage relationship. Here and now, we will attempt to keep our focus squarely on blame and deception.

All of us sin. All of us are subject to deception. We have all at one time or another blamed someone else, blamed God or claimed, in effect, 'The devil made me do it.' And so it is, that out of the four characters in the Garden of Eden, three of them are blamed for the disaster that occurred. Firstly, Eve is blamed. Then God. Lastly, the serpent is blamed. Who was in fact to blame? Scripture tells us "...sin came into the world through one man...." (Rom.5:12).

The one who was held, primarily, to blame for this catastrophe was Adam, and yet he is the one who escaped being listed as at fault. The fact that Adam is held to blame is theologically important because all humanity, including Eve, originated from this one man. And as things went wrong through the one, original man, they were therefore put right through one man, the "second Adam," Jesus Christ. "For just as through the disobedience of the one man the many were made sinners, so also through the obedience of the one man the many will be made righteous" (Rom.5:19 NIV).

However, Eve was not entirely blameless in this event. She was deceived into thinking less of God than he is, and she acted on it. Adam was there at the time, but he said nothing at all. Neither of them consulted God as to the truth of what the serpent was saying. Was it the serpent's fault? Not entirely, he just set up the possibilities. We may be tempted, but we do not have to sin. Was it God's fault for allowing this scenario to happen in the first place? Surely not.

In Scripture we find that God generously gives wisdom when asked, and he provides the means of putting things right. He doesn't encourage things to go wrong. "No one, when tempted, should say, 'I am being tempted by God' for God cannot be tempted by evil, and he himself tempts no one. But one is tempted by one's own desire, being lured and enticed by it; then, when that desire has conceived, it gives birth to sin, and that sin, when it is fully-grown, gives birth to death. Do not be deceived, my beloved" (Js 1:13–16). Eve was at fault for being deceived. Adam was not deceived, and he was held accountable for eating the fruit—"…and he ate. Then the eyes of both were opened…" (Gen 3:6–7).

WAS IT OUR FAULT?

Why do we want to blame someone else for our shortcomings? As discussed in the previous study, we feel the guilt and want to escape both the shame, and the consequences of our actions. It has to be somebody else's fault. It feels better to shift all of that uncomfortable stuff elsewhere. And so, we find that neither of the first two people to walk the earth, wanted to take responsibility. And through the sin of the "one man", "so death spread to all because all have sinned…" (Rom 5:12). We are all accountable to God for our own sin. And the guilt and shame we should feel for that should drive us to God to ask his forgiveness. 'I stuffed up. You are right and I am wrong. I am so sorry. Please forgive me.'

However, sometimes bad situations occur for which we

were not responsible. And just as we can take on board shame that is not ours to wear, so also, we can take the blame for things that we did not initiate. The key to this devilish transfer is deception. We can be deceived and blame ourselves for things that are not our fault. And we become trapped in false guilt and poor self-esteem. 'Why can't I get it right?' 'It's all my fault.'

In relation to domestic violence, Pamela Cooper-White writes: "Batterers have a very difficult time accepting responsibility for their own negative behaviour. They seek to place blame outside themselves and generally minimize and deny violent acts that they have committed." She continues that this "combined with the battered partner's over-responsibility and self-blame, tends to keep the reality and magnitude of the abuse hidden, even from the consciousness of the partners themselves much of the time."[1]

Here, in this type of situation, the woman is deceived into thinking that what has happened is her fault. She may have been told so many times that she is to blame that she is brainwashed into believing it to be true. How many women navigate the terror of potential violence within the home by desperately trying not to 'rock the boat.' Taking responsibility for maintaining an even keel in the relationship, she deems it her own fault when things explode, yet again.

As for children, if a parent offends against them, they have no reason to know things should be otherwise. As Pamela Cooper-White explains, "Children... developmentally cannot imagine another reality, another worldview than that of their parents. The parents literally define what is real and what is not. If a perpetrator says, 'This never happened,' or

---

1   Pamela Cooper-White, *The Cry of Tamar*, 120, 208.

'This is for your own good,' or 'You asked for it'—and there is no other adult in the environment where the abuse is happening who can perceive the abuse and intervene—a child has no developmental capacity even to think that life could be otherwise."[2] And so the child may take the blame onto themselves, perhaps for a lifetime.

Distressingly, we are told: "In almost all cases, male perpetrators [of child sexual abuse] deny and minimize their responsibility...Like rapists, they blame the victim, saying that she was too sexy, or that she never said no, or that she really wanted it."[3]

What hope do we have? We feel powerless in the face of these false accusations. How do we respond? Sometimes we hit back in hot defence, but often this is not possible. It may not be safe to do so, nor necessarily helpful for all sorts of reasons. And even if we did, we would somehow find ourselves supposedly in the wrong, being left without a leg to stand on. The unfairness burns deep. Feelings of dismay, helplessness, anger, rage, among many others jostle one another as we try to make sense of the situation, and search for justice.

THE DEVILISHNESS OF DECEPTION

In the Garden of Eden, we see the pattern for the first deception, for it is here the strategy of Satan is clearly depicted. This was to slightly twist the truth, causing Eve to doubt the character of God. It was inferred that God was holding something back from her. If Satan can tempt people to doubt the God in whom they have put their faith, then faith wavers. The relationship

---

2 Pamela Cooper-White, *The Cry of Tamar*, 149.

3 Pamela Cooper-White, *The Cry of Tamar*, 165.

between God and the individual is therefore compromised. Why would Satan want to do this? It is because he hates God with a passion, and he can hurt God most by destroying the object of God's love, humanity.

Dan Allender, in his essay on The Mark of Evil writes: "The evil one cannot destroy God, but he can mar, distort, and nearly destroy the mark of God in creation. For that reason, his fury and hatred are spent against human beings who are made in the image of God and bear the mark of His glory more than any other created being (Ps 8:5)."[4]

This is why wherever we see the breakdown of relationships within which new life is engendered and protected (a marriage), we can assume that Satan is at work. Disruption of living loving relationship between individuals and God, and the disruption of relationship between people is his aim. The more confusion and distress he can cause with the family or the community, and between God and his creation, the more satisfied he is. And so, he aims to blind us to the truth, and lock us up in a web of shame and blame that we think is our own doing.

"Evil works to sever relationships and destroy trust. It seeks to isolate the victim in order to gain power and destroy the intimacy and joy of connected, caring relationships. Evil refuses to allow anyone the intimacy that it has forsaken with God."[5]

---

[4] Dan B. Allender, 'The Mark of Evil' in *God and the Victim*, 39.

[5] Dan B. Allender, 'The Mark of Evil' in *God and the Victim*, 49.

THE VORACIOUSNESS OF EVIL

This hatred also in some way feeds Satan. It gives him energy he needs in order to sustain himself. We ourselves know how we can be tempted to gobble up tasty bits of gossip where others are shown to be failing. We can then feel a bit better about ourselves. It is like food to our fallen souls. Satan himself, through his own sin, is cut off from God, the source of all life. And so, he feeds himself on his hatred of God, and on those made in God's image.

How did the serpent feel about being accused in the Garden of Eden? He would undoubtedly have felt delighted. His plan had succeeded with stunning effect. His effort to deceive Eve, which led to Adam's sin were fully rewarded. And its fruit was immediately obvious. Whose fault was it? The serpent's for deceiving, or Eve's for being deceived? All the serpent did was speak some words. However, the words are used in such a way that they mean something other than what they say. 'Did I hurt you?' may be asked with genuine concern, but coming from the mouth of a deceiver, driven by a mocking spirit, it takes on a whole different meaning.

"Evil parades as light. It offers help when it desires to destroy. It sings praise when it really despises. It encourages when it actually taunts. The result is overwhelming chaos, confusion, and not only pain but also a kind of craziness which tragically presumes that somehow the victim is not really a victim but is at fault for the crime"[6] Perhaps you are puzzled by this quote, but if you have been subject to deception, and particularly if you have been brainwashed into believing lies

---

6   Dan B. Allender, 'The Mark of Evil' in *God and the Victim*, 46.

about yourself that cause you to question your sanity, you will recognise the truth of Dan Allender's statement.

STOLEN GOODS

As with Satan, the perpetrator who deliberately sets out to deceive their victim is intent on stealing something from them. With the devil, he wants to steal life itself. And if we live, he seeks to steal, wreck, or mar any loving relationship. His aim is for people to live lives unconnected to God, and in fear of death. A human deceiver may set out to steal material items such as money, or property. However, he or she is just as much a thief when integrity, self-respect, a sense of security, trust in others, and innocence are stolen.

Having been deceived, we find ourselves betrayed. We have been set up, offended against, and discarded. Our trusting nature is ridiculed, and mocked, and we are left feeling cheated, dirty and ashamed of our naivety. Over and again we are made to feel gullible and belittled. We ask ourselves, "How could I have been so stupid? If I had not been so stupid it wouldn't have happened.' We take the blame to ourselves and may even curse ourselves as we vow, 'I am never going to be so trusting ever again.' Everything is turned on its head, and the perpetrator is fed, in some way, by the distress that they cause.

WHAT HOPE IS THERE FOR US?

We may not even notice when we deceive ourselves, but at the hands of others we feel ill-equipped to recognise deceptions and deal with them as they deserve. What redress do we have? When appalling abuses of power occur, when we ourselves are sinned against, what do we choose to believe about God, and to whom do we look for help? In section one of these studies we were challenged to have an accurate understanding of God because it is foundational to our healing. Here, once again it is in Christ Jesus that we find the answers to the unfairnesses of blame and deception.

We find that if we are truly to blame, we can look to Jesus for forgiveness, so that before God we can be considered blameless. We also find that if we have been wrongly blamed, we will be vindicated and eventually granted justice. Scripture demonstrates to us that those who deceive others will themselves be deceived, and it tells us that God will restore and rebuild our lives if we turn to him. If we have deceived ourselves Jesus said, "If you continue in my word, you are truly my disciples; and you will know the truth, and the truth will make you free" (Jn 8:31–32).

We can also look to each other for help. Adam and Eve were gifted with language so that they could share their thoughts. No other creature has this ability to communicate at this level. Yet when faced with deception they neither spoke with each other, or checked with God. Surely this demonstrates to us that in the face of deception we need to talk with other Christians and gain another perspective. The necessary gifts for discernment have been gifted to the Church if we would but use them in Christian community.

As I was writing this particular study, a chaplain of a nursing home told me of an elderly woman who had recently shared something of her story. She told how, as a young woman, she was raped at gunpoint by her husband. She finally left him and re-married and lived a full Christian life, but she, herself, had always felt guilty about the rape. Fortunately, the chaplain was able to reframe the event for her, and her feelings of guilt were relieved. This wrong understanding concerning what had happened to her had stolen her peace of mind for many, many years. Talking it over with someone had enabled her to see things in a different light, which had led to her freedom.

In conversation on Sunday morning at church, I was challenged to think of the emphasis always being on our own sinfulness, and how this might make it more difficult for people struggling with inappropriate self-blame to approach God. Our current emphasis, in this project, is to think rightly about ourselves. What does God have to say about us? He came to rescue and restore because he loves us. Let's press on with our exploration of his word to us with anticipation as to the treasure we will uncover.

QUESTIONS

1. Sometimes we are rightly to blame for wrongdoing, sometimes wrongly to blame.

    - Read Genesis 3:8–13; Isaiah 53:4–9; Ezekiel 18:19–20; and 1 John 1:8–9.

    a) Who does God say is responsible for their actions?

    b) Have you ever tried to dodge the blame for something that was your own fault? Why?

    c) Have you ever consciously decided to take the blame for something that was not your fault? If so, why?

    d) Who will take the blame for your own wrongdoing, if you own up to God for it?

    e) Could there be any situation where a person is not to be held responsible for something they did or said? Why or why not?

2. Jesus was betrayed, and money changed hands. He was set up, wrongly accused, and the people turned against him. He suffered and died without defending himself.

    - Read Matthew 26:47–50; 27:11–14, 21–23; and Revelation 20:11–15.

    a) Has anyone ever accused you of something that you had not done, nor spoken, nor thought? How did you feel? What, if anything, did you, or could you, do about it?

b) How do you think God feels, when you are wrongly accused, and cannot defend yourself?

c) What comfort is it—if any—to know that it may only be God himself who ever knows the truth of the matter?

d) What comfort is it—if any—to know that your accusers will eventually face God's judgment?

3. The thread of deception runs right through all the patriarchal families in Genesis. In the third generation, Jacob, later called Israel, deceived his father, in order to inherit his brother Esau's birthright. Jacob himself was later cruelly deceived by his father-in-law and ten of his own sons.
   - Read Genesis 27: 21–25; 29:21–25; 37:29–35; John 14:6–7; Acts 5:1–11; 2 Corinthians 11:3–4; and Ephesians 4:25–27.

   a) Why do you think deception is abhorrent to God?

   b) Do you think Jacob got what he deserved? Why or why not?

   c) Who does Scripture say was behind the deception that Ananias and Saphira practised?

   d) What warnings do we all receive from reading these verses?

4. Satan's aim is to separate us from the knowledge of the love of God that he himself disdained, and to separate us from each other. Deception is his weapon.

- Read Genesis 3:1–5; John 8:42–45; 2 Corinthians 4:3–4; and 2 Thessalonians 2:9–10.

    a) Have you ever been given reason to doubt God's character, causing you to give up on him? If so, what were the circumstances?

    b) Have you ever been given reason to doubt someone else's character? If so, how?

    c) Have you ever been made to feel that God has given up on you? If so, how?

    d) According to these Bible references, how does the devil go about promoting doubt in God?

    e) Where can we hope to gain truth concerning these matters?

5. We are deceived because someone wants to steal something from us. And it is hard to recognise when we have wrongly taken blame to ourselves for something that was not our fault. But if we can lay the blame where it belongs, we can start to take account of what was stolen.

    A poem, written by a survivor of abuse at the hands of Catholic priests, Marian Lovelace, identifies both who was responsible for the abuse, and the losses she sustained, as she has come to realise that she did not lose these things—which could be deemed her fault—rather, they were stolen from her.[7] Her poem starts:

---

[7] As quoted in Marie Fortune's book, *Sexual Violence*, 70-71.

> I learned a valuable lesson today about responsibility.
>
> I now know where to leave the shame and blame.
>
> I am beginning to discover the truth–
>
> Many of my precious gifts were stolen, not lost!

She goes on to identify and list some of the many precious gifts that had been stolen from her, including her innocence, her relationship with God, her love of life, and her voice.

a) If you have not done so before, find someone safe to talk to who can help you to see your story from a different point of view. You do not need someone to tell you what you must see or do, but someone who will enable you to reframe your own picture.

b) Spend some time carefully thinking through what has been stolen from you.

c) Keep a memo pad handy to list these losses. Recognition of them may take place over a significant period of time. We will address these losses in Study 14.

If you have never consciously grieved these losses, you may have done so unconsciously. This grief can manifest in depression or other mental health issues.

You may benefit from the help of a skilled counsellor or psychologist in identifying and dealing with these griefs.

6. This distressing web of shame, blame and deception takes time to untangle. We stand dazed amid our losses and wonder where to go from here. God, however, does not just open our eyes to the truth and free us from the lies that have entrapped us. He can now begin our restoration and rebuilding into the people we were originally intended to be.

   - Read John 8:31–32; Psalm 23:1–3; Jeremiah 31:1–14; and 1 Peter 5:8–11.

   a) What is the starting point for restoration?

   b) Which of the blessings appearing in any of the readings, particularly catches your attention? Why?

   c) Share with the group any restoration and rebuilding of your own identity that you are aware of, which has already taken place in your life.

   d) What are you most hoping for, in your own life, as you journey with Jesus?

STUDY 10: SILENCE IS GOLDEN?

I was a week late joining my Pastoral Skills class. The lecturer had already sorted people into groups who were to research a particular aspect of pastoral care, and I was directed to join the 'abuse' group. Great. The students within this group had already chosen one aspect of abuse to research for their main essay and to present to the class. The topic that no one else had picked up, and which was therefore left for me, was sexual abuse. Wonderful! Had I arrived at the start of the course would I have chosen this topic? No indeed.

Why is it that this topic is one we would rather not explore? It seems that of all the types of abuse that abound, sexual abuse generates the most shame, rightly for the perpetrator but unfairly for the survivor. As discussed in Study 8, the shame that rightly belongs with the offender, sticks like glue to their victim. This abuse is therefore the one most likely to not be spoken about. For me, it was even embarrassing to be required to present my findings on the subject, that is how much I did not want to talk about it.

Fortunately, attitudes are changing, and there is much more openness and willingness to discuss what was formerly taboo. Unfortunately, this means that we, as a society, discover that this form of abuse is by no means rare. This is what I discovered in my research in 2005. I was stunned as I read in book after book after book the shocking statistics that were then known to counsellors, psychologists and pastors worldwide. Between a quarter and a third of all girls under the age of 18 are known to have been sexually abused. One in six of all girls have been subject to incestuous sexual abuse. One in three women have been raped in their lifetime.[1] Neither do boys and men escape this form of abuse. Why had I not heard of this before? Why had I never heard the topic addressed in Church, the one place where there should be refuge and healing?

I am wiser now, and so is this country. Adult survivors finally have a voice, and they are beginning to use it. However, I also have learnt that this is no easy topic to address. The secrecy of the act, the fact that children are all-too-often the victims, and the fact that this mostly happens within the circle of family and family friends, provides a scenario fraught with difficulties. There is also no simple means to bring justice to offenders, and no means for them to restore what was stolen. And as an added complication, it is also, unfortunately, possible to make accusations that may be false, that can destroy someone's good standing in community.

A CHILD'S SILENCE

While adults are beginning to come forward, difficulties persist for a child. Who believes a child? Studies reveal that a child's report of abusive behaviour will be disbelieved or discounted many times before they find someone who will believe them. Pamela Cooper-White explains: "When faced with a contest of loyalty between a distressed child or angry adolescent, and an adult whose words seem mature and reasonable, even a

---

[1] See Pamela Cooper-White, *The Cry of Tamar*, 80, 152.

sensitive and educated parent or other caretaker usually finds it difficult to stand with the child."[2] If the abuse is not shared at the time, and believed and acted upon, it may be many years later before, as an adult, the survivor can speak out and expect to be heard.

Just recently, a friend shared the story of two young girls, of which she was the first. At between four and five years old she was sexually interfered with a number of times by the next-door neighbour in his garage, the windows of which had been carefully blacked out. When she told her parents, her father, for whatever reason, did nothing. It was her mother who confronted the man and believed his story of innocence. She then labelled her daughter an attention seeking little liar. This story, and the tag that went with it, was passed on by the perpetrator's wife to the wife of the local store owner, who would not allow the "dirty little liar" into the shop, but made her stand outside.

The offender then turned his attention to a second young girl in the street. However, her father responded differently. He believed his daughter's story and took to his neighbour with a long-handled shovel! Both girls suffered the same abuse, but it is not difficult to imagine which one suffered most and for the longest. The perpetrator continued living next door to my friend for the next twenty years.

With incestuous abuse, how is the child to know that this isn't what life is supposed to be like? As we discovered in the previous study, children do not have the cognitive ability to imagine that things might be any different in another family.[3] They are therefore stuck, confused and perplexed. They are

---

[2] Pamela Cooper-White, *The Cry of Tamar*, 147.

[3] Pamela Cooper-White, *The Cry of Tamar*, 149.

without a voice and without help. How does this helplessness in the face of such trauma unconsciously shape their thinking? How can they express their distress?

When reviewing the local craft work in an up-market souvenir shop recently, I noticed some small fabric teddies. What caught my attention was the fact that they had each had eyes and nose embroidered for their face, but none of them had been given a mouth. I was wondering about the artist, and what her story might have been. No mouth means no voice.

WHY NOT SHARE?

It is natural for the offended soul of a person to want to be heard, to want to be believed, and to want to bring to the light the unfairness of the shameful things that were done in secrecy. It is right to seek justice, and desire to protect others from what was done to them. So why would a survivor not share their story?

Every situation is unique and complex. On thinking this through, I very quickly managed to list more than half a dozen different reasons for keeping silent. Top of the list must surely be fear. Fear for his or her life; fear of being assaulted again, or even killed; fear of not being believed; fear of rejection; fear of the consequences of supposedly having done something wrong; fear of exile from community; fear of loss of parents. How distressing it was to view a documentary, recently, where children were rescued from their mothers who were selling their children's bodies for sex. The child clings to the mother.

Another reason for not sharing is shame, and maybe a feeling, or even strong belief for the survivor, that they were themselves in some way to blame. Yet another reason concerns other loved ones. Does the survivor want to protect someone else from the truth? In circumstances of incest, an older child may feel it would break their mother's heart to know such stuff about her husband, or brother, or son, or father. And yet another facet of protecting others from the truth is not wanting to burden others with your story. Can they cope? Do they need to know? Would their hearts break on your account? Do they need particular details, or just a general outline that something happened way back in childhood?

And yet another reason concerns the potential hearer. Not everyone can be trusted with such revelation. An inability to keep a confidence disqualifies a potential confidante. Horrified interest in specifics rightfully has the door shut in its face. We do not share with people who are too ready with (mis)judgments, or solutions, or inappropriate instructions such as 'You must forgive and forget.' And the response: 'I know just what you are talking about' prompts an immediate, though not always spoken, 'No you don't.' Besides, such a response signals that the other is more ready to talk about themselves than listen to anything you might have liked to have shared.

KEEPING A SECRET FROM YOURSELF

The ultimate in silence and isolation is to keep the secret from yourself, for you cannot call out for help or share your story if you cannot recall it. The mind of a child can play a clever trick and split off the horror of the abuse from the conscious mind. This enables them to hide away the truth so that they cannot recall the terrifying circumstances of being abused by the one(s) on whom they are dependant for survival. "The younger the child at the time of onset of abuse and the greater the dependency, the deeper this split and the more delusional its intensity."[4] This process is known as repression, which allows the child to survive in an overwhelmingly awful, ongoing situation. Survivors may also dissociate during the abuse, absenting their conscious mind from the experience, thus cushioning the impact of the mental and physical pain of the event.

Everyone represses memories and everyone dissociates. They are normal, and common phenomena that are engaged in daily. We may not hear someone call our name because our mind is elsewhere at the time. We do not consciously remember every detail of every event in our daily life because we simply could not cope with the wealth of information. However, disturbing memories may be more deeply buried.

A continuum of increasingly profound division of memories into separate compartments may exist. These range from a relatively easily accessible inner child, to the formation of entirely separate personalities resulting from the unspeakable torture and atrocities of ritual abuse.[5] Although hidden, these memories, if sustained in childhood, may begin to emerge later in life as the repressive mechanisms begin to weaken. It is then that they may need to be acknowledged and dealt with.

A NEED TO BE HEARD

There are therefore seemingly any number of reasons a person may feel unable to call out for help, be unable to share their distress, or may feel unheard, if they have indeed made the attempt to speak up. An inability to share, for whatever reason, leaves the survivor isolated in their own grief. In this

---

[4] Pamela Cooper-White, *The Cry of Tamar*, 150.

[5] See Pamela Cooper-White, *The Cry of Tamar*, 157–160, 169–182; Charles H. Kraft, *Deep Wounds Deep Healing*, 228.

place of isolation, it is all too easy to take on the blame and the shame of the abusive events and to spiral into sadness, depression and low self-esteem. The release, therefore, when discovering that you are not the only one to suffer such abuse, can be dramatic.

One woman, on reading just a short paragraph from a chapter on domestic violence says she took it home and danced round her living room, waving the written text in the air. The writer had so precisely expressed the dynamics of her relationship with her former husband that it was as if she had been 'heard' for the first time. Furthermore, as it was written by a pastor who worked with many such abused women, and it was printed in a book, it must mean that there were possibly thousands of women who had suffered just as she had. She was not alone, and she could begin to consider that what had happened to her was not her fault!

One of the most useful, practical things I learnt during my pastoral studies was that people need to be given the opportunity to be heard. This does not require my finding answers to their problems, or sharing my own with them, it requires me to listen, and listen carefully. I do not, of course, always accomplish this aim, but at least I am aware of the necessity to try. It is a skill in high demand in our community considering the extent of the need.

Given the known statistics, at least a third of all women, and a significant number of men in any church congregation, will have been subject to some form of sexual abuse in their lifetime. If other forms of abuse are also included, the percentages rise accordingly. If the silence is broken, we can help each other. The need for Christians to be present and available to simply hear people's stories cannot be understated. Likewise, the value of survivors in being available for each other can be immeasurable. This is because it is among these people that we find those who do know what it is like to suffer, survive, and maybe also move on to victory over the circumstances that caused such grief and loss.

GOD HEARS US

As Christians, of course, we have access to comfort and understanding that is individually tailored to our own specific needs. For each one of us who have stories we cannot, for one reason or another share, there is immeasurable comfort in knowing that God himself knows our story and hears our cries, and will, in the fullness of time, wipe away all of our tears. Justice will be dispensed, and the truth will be known.

If we were ever to wonder if God wanted to hear from us, we have only to look at the Psalms. Scripture is God's word to us, so it is a wonder that in the centre of the Bible are one hundred and fifty songs addressed by believers to God. In these songs are registered all the emotions a person can experience. Worship and adoration jostle with hate and vindictiveness.

By including them in his word, God is giving us permission to do likewise. We find it is OK to express these powerful emotions to him. His shoulders are broad enough to welcome the praise with the puzzlement; the bewilderment with the adoration. He will not take offence. He knows how we feel anyway, so it is obviously for our own good that we express ourselves honestly before him and speak out the truth of where we are at.

At the time of writing, my eldest grandson was a toddler, two and a half years old. At that age he tended to just go walking off on a mission of his own without regard for the direction the family were heading. On one occasion we were walking in a park alongside a beach when he took off. I followed a few steps behind and let him go, wondering how far he would travel without reference to the rest of us.

On and on he went, steadily walking the wrong way along the path, weaving his way between pedestrians and pushchairs. I didn't take my eyes from him for a moment, but he didn't know I was there. If he had called out or cried, I would have been with him in an instant. Eventually he happened to turn around and saw me. His face lit up. "Hello Grandma. You found me!", he said. He then happily took my hand and walked back the way we had come. I had, of course, never lost him. And in just the same way does God keep his eye on us. We are never alone, never unwatched, never unheard.

I love reading the first part of Psalm 18 where David calls out in distress to God, and God hears him and responds. Rather like the father with the long-handled shovel, he comes thundering out of heaven, deals with the enemy then reaches down and rescues his son, delivering him to a safe broad place "because he delighted in me". May God continue to rescue us and deliver us to a broad safe place. We don't need to tell him anything. Even if we ourselves have forgotten, he knows it all.

QUESTIONS

1. Sometimes we feel we have no voice, for various reasons.
   - Read Genesis 39:6–20; Job 13:1–5; Isaiah 53:7; and Matthew 26:59–68.

   a) In Joseph's story, we read that having been wrongly accused, he is given no opportunity to defend himself but is cast into prison. Can you identify with any part of Joseph's story? If so, how did it affect you?

   b) Job, who has suffered greatly through no fault of his own, has endured sustained reprimands from two of his friends. Can you understand why he had such an angry outburst toward them?

   c) Have you ever been in a similar situation with friends or family? If so, how did you respond?

   d) Why do you think Jesus initially kept silent when brought before the Jewish court? What happened when he did speak out truth?

   e) Have you ever shared your side of your story with anyone? Why or why not?

2. As Christians we are instructed to look out for each other.
   - Read Job 2:11–13; John 13:34–35; Romans 12:9–18; 2 Corinthians 1:3–7;

a) List all the things that Job's friends initially did right toward him. Do you have any experience you can share of family or friends behaving toward you in this way?

b) Make a mental list of all the people (if any) who have come alongside you and helped you along the way. What is it about them that you most value?

c) What comfort do you think you can provide to others who have suffered abuse?

d) In what practical ways can we bear one another's burdens?

3. Right in the centre of God's Word to us is a whole book devoted to what we, his followers, have said to him. By including all of these songs in the Bible, God, in effect, gives permission to all of us to speak out to him what is in our hearts.

- Read Psalm 13:1–2; 22:1–5: 44:23–26; and 137:7–9;

a) What strong emotions can you find expressed in these psalms?

b) Are you surprised or puzzled by any of the statements you see included here? If so, why?

c) Do any of these verses resonate with your feelings? If so, how?

d) Some of these verses seem to find fault with God. What are your thoughts about this?

e) How helpful is it to know that it is safe to pour out

your true feelings to God, concerning him and the people who have hurt you?

4. Psalm 147:5 tells us that God's understanding is beyond measure. Immediately following this statement, we are told that God lifts up the downtrodden, and treads down the wicked. God understands. And he understands everything.

- Read Psalm 10:17–18; 18:4–6, 17–18; 56:8; 139:1–4; John 2:24–25; and Rev 7:16–17.

    a) What confidence do you have in knowing that God believes your story?

    b) Even if you yourself cannot fully recall all the details of your own story, how can you be sure that God has not missed, nor forgotten, one detail of it?

    c) What comfort do you have in knowing that God fully understands your situation?

    d) What does God promise into the future for you, if you have trusted in him?

5. You may be isolated in your grief, unable to share with anyone.

- Read Genesis 12:10–20; 21:8–10, 14–19; 34:1–7, 25–26; 37:18–24; and Jeremiah 38:1–6.

    a) Which of these stories resonates most strongly with you, and why?

    b) In the story you chose above, what particular griefs would the character have been dealing with?

c) In the narrative, not one of these characters is given a voice to defend themselves, they are silent. What could you imagine them saying, if they had been given a chance?

d) Hagar enters into conversation with God (Gen 21:17). She and her son are sustained and promised a future. How do you imagine your voice will be heard, into the future?

SECTION THREE: ABOUT HOW WE RELATE TO OTHERS

STUDY 11: WHERE THE RUBBER HITS THE ROAD

There is a command in Hebrews that always comes to my mind as "strive to enter that rest." The Amplified Bible translates this phrase as "Let us therefore be zealous and exert ourselves and strive diligently to enter that rest [of God, to know and experience it for ourselves]... (Heb.4:11). It sticks in the mind because it seems so odd to have to work really hard to enter into rest. What is this rest that we must not miss out on? The writer is speaking of the sabbath rest of God after creation, and of the entering of the promised land by the Israelites led by Joshua. This rest I am to strive for cannot be heaven itself, for we do not get to heaven by works but by faith in God.

It could be understood as putting our faith in God. If we have trusted ourselves to Christ, we gain a measure of rest knowing we are in him, and yet that is not the end of the story, it is just the beginning, for we don't then go on holiday until we graduate to heaven. So perhaps there is also an unfolding rest in God that we are urged to attain here on earth. A rest where we are at peace with God, secure in the full knowledge of his love and provision for us; at peace with ourselves and our past; confident in our future; and at peace with how we relate to others. A rest where I can just be me, and not mind being the me I am. But I, myself, am not there yet. This is seemingly going to be very hard work!

So far, the challenge in this series of studies has been to reconsider who we think God is. Was the image of our own making, or did it line up with what the Bible tells us about him? Then we came to consider our wounds and the complex dynamics of the effects of abuse on a person. However, as it is in relationship that we were wounded, it is back in relationship where the rubber hits the road. This is because how we relate to others is where we see the fruit of our efforts to understand God, and his heart toward us, more correctly. And it is where we see the fruit of our efforts in identifying and yielding up to God our wounds for healing. If our efforts do not generate a change in how we relate to God, to others in our family, or community, or to fellow Christians, they may have been in vain.

THE STRUGGLE

What are we struggling with in our relating at the moment? In Christian circles, forgiveness and reconciliation always spring to mind. We will be considering these in later studies, along with other particular challenges that may arise for survivors of abuse. Here, in this study, we are considering difficulties that may exist within our current, day to day relationships. All of us engage in a bit of a spiritual workout every day as we navigate our interactions with other people. For those of us who have suffered abuse, however, the challenges may be more intense.

Why? Because we know we should be more gracious, not so needy, not such a doormat, more of this, less of that. Perhaps rigidly self-reliant, we find it impossible to delegate. We refuse help, refuse gifts, refuse relationship. Maybe we struggle and squirm worrying about what people think about us, or why we said such and such. Riddled with embarrassment, or desperate to be assured we did OK, we use up quantities of energy trying to manage our wounded selves. We are certainly not 'resting.' Where do we begin in trying to understand why it is so difficult for us to navigate life? Other people seem to manage it without jumping through hoops. Why can't I?

OUR BEGINNINGS SHAPE OUR THINKING

Where do we begin? At the start of our own story, beginning with our birth, because it is in the first years of life that the programming that governs our responses to others is initially wired into place. When was the last time you held a newborn baby? This utterly helpless little person is dependent for everything on older and wiser human beings, who hopefully have a care for them. How do they manage to get what they need? From their point of view, they can only cry out their need, whether it be food, comfort or companionship. If and when and how these needs are met, begin to shape the way that they relate to significant others in their lives.

Everything depends on having their needs met. They cannot go and prepare their own lunch or use the toilet. As they grow older, by trial and error they will work out what behaviour works best in the circumstances they find themselves. We may not remember how we were cared for as a young child, but the way in which our infant minds adapted our behaviour in order to have our needs met, set the template for future relationships.

Dr. Tim Clinton and Dr. Gary Sibcy usefully summarise research into this phenomenon which they term "attachment styles" in their book Attachments.[1] The research shows that in navigating infanthood, the answers to self-focused thoughts such as 'Am I capable of getting the love and support I need?' and 'Am I worthy of having my needs met?' emerge, together with carer-focused questions such as, 'Are others capable of caring for me?' and 'Are they capable but unwilling to care for me?' One way or another, according to their own answers to these questions, the child eventually decides that if their needs are not readily met it was either their own fault, or their carer's fault, or both. They will then decide they will manage by themselves or be very clingy. Or perhaps they alternate between the two.

The ideal, of course, is that the child learns that their needs are readily and lovingly met. And they deduce that they are capable of obtaining what they need and are worthy of that attention. In addition, they deduce that their carers are both capable and willing to provide for these needs. And so it is that they become securely attached to their parents, resting in the confidence that this situation brings. Thus in a perfect world, Mum and Dad model the love and care of God for the child. In due course, as the child matures, this attachment is transferred to God who has always loved them unconditionally, and is ready, willing and able to fully meet all their needs as they turn to him.

THE WIRING IS IN PLACE

However, we don't live in a perfect world, and the abuse

---

[1] Tim Clinton and Gary Sibcy, *Attachments*.

that many of us have endured at some point in our lives further complicates the matter. As adults, we still have our felt needs and we still look to have these needs met. The bottom line governing our behaviour is still to maximise pleasure and minimise pain.[2] As we set out on life's journey, our programming kicks in and we pursue our relationships according to the pattern we taught ourselves as a child. Only as survivors of abuse the effects of any insecurity are multiplied, and the resultant distress is intensified.

We quickly, and unconsciously learn that if we are to survive, we will need to have a public face, a way of interacting with others socially, that is acceptable to others, in order to gain what we think we need. All the other stuff we hide away, sometimes even from ourselves. After all, we can cope better without dwelling on it. We tell ourselves it was our fault anyway, we deserved it, or it didn't matter (we can't afford to let it matter). Or it's only what happens to many others and they manage somehow. As Allender explains, we need to deaden the pain of soul hunger, while being alert to acting in our own best interests. Our heart is dull to its own pain.[3] It can't feel a thing. And yet it is still shaping our behaviour.

OUR PUBLIC FACES

What are these different public faces we display to the world? Allender describes three very generalised types for women who have been subject to sexual abuse, but they could arise in response to other wounds.[4] He sketches a Good Girl, a "peace

---

2 Dan B. Allender, *Wounded Heart*, 89.

3 Dan B. Allender, *Wounded Heart*, 89.

4 Dan B. Allender, *Wounded Heart*, 160–170.

at any price" way of relating that refuses to impose on others. Then is there the Tough Girl, who "is and will be in charge." Her self-protective behaviour is so strongly structured as to keep everyone from touching her soul. Lastly, Allender describes the Party Girl, whose relationships are always superficial and selfish, gobbling up whatever she can get from those around her, before moving on.

In a similar vein, John Eldredge, in his book Wild at Heart, talks of wounded men "faking" their way through life. Their public face may be a macho, fist-fighting type, or a driven high achieving perfectionist, or a passive type who has decided to allow life to pass him by.[5] In each case, like women, they are hiding their true self, and looking to bluster their way through life in their own self-protective, self-reliant way.

When we become Christian, there are further complications as we attempt to steer our way between the conflicting demands to love others, and our desire to avoid the pain that such a relationship could bring.[6] How do we manage? Eldredge warns, "The only thing more tragic than the tragedy that happens to us is the way we handle it."[7] What, however, are our options? We have survived so far, it's been tough, but we've done it. Isn't that the best we can do? Doesn't that deserve credit?

OUR CHALLENGE, AS CHRISTIANS

A warning is to be found in the full verse of Hebrews 4:11 with which I began this study. This reads: "Let us, therefore,

---

5 John Eldredge *Wild at Heart*, 55–57.

6 Dan B. Allender, *Wounded Heart*, "The call to love and the determination to dodge hurt set up a radical contradiction in the soul," 159.

7 John Eldredge *Wild at Heart*, 105–113.

make every effort to enter that rest, so that no one will fall by following their example of disobedience." The writer was speaking of the Israelites who failed to enter their promised land, their place of rest, on account of their disobedience. If they failed, then so can we. Is it possible that we may be handling our response to our tragedy disobediently?

The most surprising, yet helpful challenge that I have so far come across in my journey of healing has been to understand, not only that I am totally responsible for my own response to the abuse I have endured—which I already knew—but that my response has been sinful—which I hadn't realised.[8] "But that's not fair!" I cry. Not only did I suffer the abuse, I am held responsible for my response! Furthermore, if my response continues to be sinful, I am going to miss gaining that rest. I'm going to be struggling forever.

I came to see that like that of so many others who have suffered, my failing was to look to myself for my survival, instead of to God. My sin has been to look to my own efforts to maximise comfort and minimise pain. And it is so subtle, and so much a part of how I have managed life that I can't even see it, unless God points it out to me. The wiring is there. Just flick the switch and I move into self-protective mode.

Only yesterday God pointed out to me that I have already rationalised a strategy for coping with the potential disappointment of not completing this book. I already have a cushion in place, should I find myself falling, or failing. I then understood my reason for being unwilling to read a story unless I know it has a happy ending. I am protecting myself from the possible pain of identifying with a hero or heroine whose story ends in tragedy. I even have to check who has

---
8   Dan B. Allender, *Wounded Heart*, 26–27.

been eliminated in Masterchef before I can cope with watching the episode! What hope is there for me if I can't even see my problem?

Our hope lies in God. Our remedy is to become securely attached to our heavenly Father, God, who knows us inside out and loves us unconditionally. This means that we have to be willing to have all the faulty wiring replaced. And it means that all the junk we have shoved in the cellar, or the attic, will need an airing. He is waiting for us to take up the invitation to renovation. He will, however, do nothing without our 'Yes please.' Will we trust him? And yet we pause for careful thought.

IS THIS GOING TO HURT?

Why the hesitation? Because we sense it is going to cost us something, and it is possibly going to hurt. A dead person can feel nothing. A deadened soul has withdrawn itself, one way or another, from honest interaction with others. It refuses to feel the pain, and avoids further potential hurt. But Jesus said, "I came that they may have life, and have it abundantly" (Jn.10:10). An awakened soul braces itself to face what has long been buried, and to feel the pain of it. Dare we risk being brought back to life—being resurrected? Can we find the courage to trust God to supply all that we will need in the adventure?

It will mean looking to him for the strength to stand up for who he made us to be, and the wisdom as to how we should go about it. The one who has been a doormat decides to respectfully speak out her feelings, and politely refuses the demands made upon her, trusting to God for the outcome. The driven perfectionist looks to God for his affirmation, choosing to believe God's opinion of himself. The controller, who invests so much energy in protecting herself from being hurt, relinquishes her grip on her soul, allowing God to awaken her to her vulnerabilities and feel the warmth, and risk, of experiencing loving relationship.

Every situation is unique, and what might be excellent strategy in one case may lead to disaster in another. These are complex webs we have woven around ourselves and those we relate to, and only God knows the best way to lead us to freedom. However, whatever the strategy, the Israelites had to actually take the land God had already given them, and we are going to have to choose to be engaged in the battle to attain our rest.

Why expose ourselves to potential pain? Because Jesus came to give us life, in all its fullness, not to live a lifeless shadow of an existence, getting by using an ungodly persona who does not do justice to the vital living being we were created to be. Jesus has won the victory so that we may enter our rest. How much victory do we want? Are we content to say, "I will have just this much thank you, I don't want to upset the apple cart, rock the boat." Or do we choose to honour Christ's finished work on our behalf, and trust him to lead us into all the victory he has for us?

What are we giving up? Our self-protective, self-reliant ways of relating. What are we potentially gaining? Rest in being able to be the 'me' God designed me to be; and abundant life, life in all its fullness. We may not a have a clue what these may look like, but we only have the one life, one chance at this adventure.

QUESTIONS

1. It is very difficult for us to identify our strategy for relating to others because it is so much a part of who we are.
   - Read Psalm 28:6–7; 145:13b–20; Isaiah 26:3–4; Mark 5:15; and Romans 12:1–2.

   a) Does any of this study so far, ring true for you? If so, which parts?

   b) Do you recognise any challenges in your current relationships? Are you able to identify your strategy for coping with them?

   c) What do you think it means to be securely attached to God?

   d) What is God willing and able to do for you in any potential renovation project if you trust in him?

   e) Why would you choose to trust him with an adventure into the unknown? Why might you hesitate to do so?

2. Scripture tells us there is a sabbath rest awaiting us, which we can miss on account of unbelief.
   - Read Genesis 2:1–3; Numbers 13:25–33; 14:1–9, 24; Joshua 1:1–7, 9; and Hebrews 4:9–11.

   a) In your opinion, what does "to enter your rest" mean? What might it mean for you?

b) What dismayed all of the Israelites except Moses, Joshua and Caleb? Where was their focus?

c) What did Caleb do that opened the way for him to enter the promised land?

d) In the reading from Joshua, how many times does God command Joshua to be strong and courageous?

e) What does this tell you about the task ahead, and about God's concern for Joshua?

3. We may hide our hurts away, unacknowledged and unlooked at. This, however, hinders us from processing the grief that rightfully belongs with those wounds.
   - Read Psalm 72:12–14; Isaiah 53:1–5; 61:1–4; Daniel 2:22; Mark 4:22; and Hebrews 4:12–16.

   a) You may have forgotten abusive events, or not recognised them as abusive. Or you may have simply not acknowledged to yourself that you were abused. Who can bring these hidden memories to the light?

   b) Have you ever told yourself that an abusive event didn't matter. That is, have you told yourself that you are not going to let it affect you?

   c) Did what happened to you matter to God? In which verses do you find your answer?

   d) Finally acknowledging that you were wounded, and that it mattered, opens up the way to engaging with the grieving process. The tears can begin to flow. What are God's promises regarding your grief?

4. Our life in Christ is a journey toward more and more Christlikeness. We don't know what is coming next, or which way we should go. As we trust in him, God leads us ever onward with gentleness and grace.

    - Read Psalm 23:1–6; 103:13–14; Isaiah 40:11; 42:3; Matthew 11:28–30; and 1 Peter 5:6–7.

    a) As you step out into possibly difficult terrain, what comfort do you find in Psalm 23? Be specific.

    b) What, specifically, does the Lord undertake to provide for those who trust in him?

    c) What does Jesus, and then Peter, instruct you to do with your burdens and anxieties?

    d) How do you actually go about doing this? Help each other with your answers.

    e) From these verses, how would you sum up God's attitude toward his people?

5. There may be any number of a variety of links in the chain that have locked us into ungodly ways of relating to others. They may include:

    - Insecure attachment as an infant
    - Later woundedness
    - Not trusting God, or not looking to God to supply our needs
    - Self-defensive response
    - Self-reliant response
    - Not acknowledging that there has been any abuse
    - Not living true to your feelings (not the same as simple good manners)

- Hiding or choosing to forget the hurts / not knowing how to manage them
- Various struggles in relating, in a godly way, to others

- Read Psalm 68:6; 146:7; Isaiah 42:6–7; Zechariah 9:11–12; and Luke 4:18.

a) Can you identify any links that may be relevant to your situation?

b) If you have felt locked into certain unhelpful behaviour patterns, are you willing to be set free?

c) What would freedom look like to you? What would be your first step toward it?

d) What do you most fear about moving forward toward more wholesome relational strategy? How will you face it?

STUDY 12
MIND HOW YOU GO

As a brand new Christian, living at that time in a small country community half an hour from the nearest town, I found myself struggling to see myself as part of the local church fellowship. "They are not the sort of people I would choose to mix with socially" I confided to the pastor. It seemed to me that they were old-fashioned, 'countrified' people. There's me, a young mum, wearing my up-to-the-minute velveteen track suits (!!!), whereas the ladies seemed to favour tweed skirts and cable knit cardigans. Very wisely, the pastor suggested that I had better get used to these folk because they were the people I would be spending eternity with!

Of course, once I got to know them, and discovered their passion for Jesus, I no longer noticed what they were wearing, or their age or their (to me) old-fashioned ways. We were simply sisters and brothers in Christ, excited to share what God was doing in our lives, and keen to share him with others. I may have thought these people to be too different to myself for there to be any connection between us, but now I discovered we were family. And you don't choose family.

As it happened, many years later I found myself part of a church fellowship of about two hundred individuals in a big city. At that time, I counted at least seventeen different nationalities within the congregation, each bringing their own cultural flavour to the Church community. What a wonderful testament to the grace of God active amongst us; and surely a taste of heaven.

So it is that we find that relating to others may have its challenges whether they are in the context of having been subject to abuse or not. However, for many who have been offended against, it is because they have found themselves on the wrong side of a social, or cultural divide. Perhaps it is to do with skin colour, or maybe a size or shape issue. We may know what it is like to be stared at, picked on or ignored, taunted or rejected simply on the grounds of what we look like, or how we present ourselves to others. Culture, race, social status, employment, education, age, gender, disability, or disease may all be the occasion for abuse. Even personal history, such as known or imagined sins we are supposed to have committed, can make us the targets of those who perceive themselves to be on the right side of the divide.

Fortunately, in Christ we have learnt that none of these visible or known or imagined features matter one jot because God looks on the heart to discern our character—and the hearts of those who have offended against us. "People judge by outward appearance, but the LORD looks at a person's thoughts and intentions" (1 Sam 16:7 NLT). Of course, not everyone we need to rub shoulders with knows that! So, what might be particular challenges to us, as survivors of abuse, as we pursue Christlike behaviour toward others?

JUDGMENT

Perhaps we were not believers at the time of the offence, but now we have come to faith in Jesus Christ, we find ourselves required to identify our hurts and pursue healing. What is going to be our attitude toward those who offended against us? Jesus gives us some stern, seemingly impossible teaching in the Sermon on the Mount: "Turn the other cheek," "Love your enemies," "Be perfect!" "Forgive others their debts." "Oh no!" We cry. "Impossible!" "And not forgiveness too!".

Forgiveness might spring to mind now... And it is so crucial to our own future health and wellbeing that we devote a whole chapter to this in Study 14. But at the time of the offence(s), amidst all the confusion of emotions we ourselves were feeling, the first response toward the offender was possibly one of judgment. I don't need to document any of the judgments we might have made toward them. They spring to mind readily enough. If we haven't thought this matter through before, it is there for us to think it through now. Because also in the Sermon on the Mount, Jesus teaches us "Do not judge, so that you may not be judged. For with the judgment you make you will be judged, and the measure you give will be the measure you get" (Mt 7:1–2).

Were me made in the image of God? So were they. But they were supposed to have a care for us! We found ourselves tricked, deceived, betrayed by family or so-called friends! We found ourselves offended against, even in church, by other so-called believers! These wounds certainly hurt most because these people are surely meant to know better. But Scripture tells us that we have all, every one of us, fallen short of his glory (Rom 3:23). Which includes us.

FOUNDATIONAL TRUTHS

Scripture gives us a sure foundation for judging that we have indeed been offended against. We judge the offence. But Scripture also provides our guidelines for not judging others.

Concerning all peoples

From Genesis 2, we learn that we are all descended from the one original man, Adam, and from Eve, who was made from Adam (Gen 21–23). The genetic code for all races, shapes and sizes of people derives from one source. Later we discover that all the peoples of the earth were descendants of the three sons of Noah—Shem, Ham and Japheth—and their wives, who survived the flood (Gen 9:18). Therefore, all people can be considered equal in humanity before God, and equally precious. And all of us, no matter what our standing in the world's eyes must come through the second Adam, Jesus Christ, if we are to be reconciled with God (Rom 5:12–21).

Whatever may have happened throughout history to distort, in any way, an understanding of the equality of all people in the eyes of God, this is put right as we choose to trust in Jesus, and join the family of believers. In the New Testament, we find the Apostle Paul affirming that as believers, it makes no difference whether you are Jew or not, free or a slave, man or a woman. All are counted equally, heirs to the promises of God (Gal 3:28–29). Therefore, neither our race, our social status, nor our gender are grounds for discriminating against someone else, nor for being discriminated against.

Concerning man and woman

But perhaps we hesitate concerning men and women? Are there Scriptural grounds for thinking of men and women a little differently when it comes to equality? Weren't women made for men, as their helpers? Aren't men supposed to be the ones in charge, and women, generally, the support group? A subservient role? Our views on this topic will affect how we relate to others, whether we are male or female, and it is therefore a challenge that is common to all of us.

So, what does the Scripture say, exactly? In Gen 1:27, we are told "male and female he created them." What is revealed to us here is not only humankind created in God's image, but humankind presenting two differing facets of this image of God on earth, one male, one female. No differentiation is made here as to their status before God. Equal in dignity and purpose, they are to rule the earth, and they are to be fruitful. That is, to fill the earth with humanity.

In Genesis 2, we learn that the female was created by God, and by his hand alone, out of the male. Thus, they are of the very same substance as each other—not separate and differing types of creature. The woman could not count herself superior to the man simply because she was the completion of God's creative process. Nor could the man claim superiority on account of being made before her. In fact, all the rest of creation was made before either of them.

We gain a further glimpse of the co-equal status of these first two individuals in learning the nature of the female, which is rather unhelpfully translated as 'helper' in the English language. A father can of course help his son tie his shoelaces, but when used of womankind in the context of Genesis 2, 'helper' has often been taken to denote a servant role. Taking this view, a man is considered to be the principal character in life's drama, and the woman 'helps' him achieve his destiny.

However, the Hebrew word for helper, ezer ke-negdo, denotes a much fuller, more robust picture of original womanhood. Ezer signifies strength, even strength in battle.[1] And ke-negdo can be translated as 'corresponding to' or 'counterpart.' It infers equality. And thus, the woman can be thought of as a strong individual alongside the man, and exactly meeting his needs, as he meets hers.[2]

It is true that this relationship was seriously compromised after Adam and Eve fell into sin. However, Jesus' ministry in defeating sin, death and Satan has redeemed the situation, restoring the dynamic of male/female relationship to God's original design. In the gospels, we can see how Jesus models for us how men should interact with women, and how women can expect to interact with men. And with the coming of the Holy Spirit, we find the gifts distributed to all believers, without any reference to gender.

Of course, the marriage relationship is unique among male/female relationships. We explore the dynamic of marriage in Study 13. But whether married or not, men and women are deemed co-equal stewards of God's creation (Gen 1:27-31). And a man cannot consider himself to have authority over any woman simply because he is a man. Indeed, a man or a woman may have authority on account of their standing in society, or their position at work. In which case, either of them can expect

---

[1] Jonalyn Grace Fincher, in her detailed study of this word summarised man's helper, or 'ezer' as "a delivering, warring, supporting, shielding, capable, and vibrant female image bearer of God." *Ruby Slippers*, 66.
Ruth Haley Barton gives a similar exposition of this term in her essay 'How I changed my mind about women in leadership', in the book of the same title, 41.

[2] David Atkinson, in his commentary explains "It certainly points to one who is fit to stand before the man, opposite him, as his counterpart, companion and complement. There is no sense of inferiority, subordination or servitude implied here – rather it is one who is 'like him', but 'like opposite him' (to give a literal rendering)." *The Bible Speaks Today; The Message of Genesis 1-11*, 69.

the respect of the people they are in charge of, whether male or female.[3]

Where honour is due?

It is all very well to struggle with recognising the value before God of those who offended against us. And of not judging them. But what if the offenders included parents? Scripture informs us that we are to "Honour your father and your mother, so that your days may be long in the land that I am giving you" (Ex 20:12). How is this possible? This must be one of the trickiest hurdles to overcome as we pursue Christlikeness. How can we behave in a respectful manner toward someone who should have loved and cared for us, and instead has betrayed us?

Godly counsel will be required, and God promises to provide the wisdom and grace we need. Keeping quiet concerning any abuse we are subject to is not forbidden, but neither is it required of us. Wrongs need to be brought to the light, in order for them to be addressed. This will be most helpfully done according to God's timing and wise counsel. But how is this possible without dishonouring the parent?

Maybe God will provide unique ways for each of us to overcome this difficulty. What we do know is that we can share what was done, but we do not pronounce judgment on the one who did it. And we may express ourselves passionately, but still be unreservedly polite, and utterly truthful in our disclosures. In this way we honour not only our parent, but also God, and ourselves. Judgment, fortunately, is God's domain. He knows the full story, and he will judge accordingly. Our own health,

---

[3] There are a number of texts in the NT that may be considered contentious with respect to the ministry of women within the church. These are dealt with in a positive, scholarly and detailed way by David Joel Hamilton in the very readable book *Why not Women?*

holistically, is bound up in God's provision for forgiveness, which we tackle in Study 14.

UNHELPFUL HISTORY

That reminds me

Who wants to remember and dwell upon bad things that happen to us? Perhaps these events intrude into our conscious thought, and demand attention. But often, we tuck these memories away, undealt with. Often there seems to be no hope of justice, and we simply just want to get on with our lives. But even our unconscious mind will jolt us into remembrance. And we can run into trouble without understanding why.

Some years ago, as a member of a small group on a mission trip overseas, I kept running into difficulty with a young woman on the team. She was the age of my own children, and she was often abrupt, to the point of being rude to me. I couldn't understand what I might have done to cause such a reaction in her and eventually we sat down to prayerfully talk it over. We came to realise that I was exactly the same age as her mother, with whom she had a difficult relationship. She was unconsciously transferring all her thoughts and feelings about her mother onto me, and therefore behaving toward me as she did to her mother. This is a process called transference. Once we identified the problem, things improved and we became good friends.

So here it is that we find another complication as survivors, an extra mile that we have to go. For we find we not only have difficulty in working out how we are to relate to people who have offended against us. We also find difficulty in relating to people who remind us of them. And very often, or perhaps even most of the time, we don't notice our own behaviour.

A challenge common to many Christians, as survivors, pivots on this very issue of transference. How many people find it impossible to relate to God as Father, or perhaps even relate to him as a male? I did so, myself, without understanding why. I would pray to Jesus, but not to Father God. This may be because, unconsciously, we have transferred what we know of fathers, or absent fathers, to God himself. And we expect from God what we received, or didn't receive, while we were growing up. We imagine an inaccurate image of God, and therefore adopt an unhelpful attitude toward him.[4] And so the challenge is there. Are we willing to explore the possibility of knowing God in this role? Are we willing to explore what being properly 'fathered' really means?

A bit of a shock

This issue of fatherhood, or parenthood, can cause many people difficulties, because most often, intergenerational issues originate in the home. This is because, as we have discussed previously, it is where children are most vulnerable. Thus the celebration of Mother's Day and Father's Day in a church service can be like a minefield for those who have suffered within their family. One Father's Day, as I entered church, I was faced with what most people would consider to be a beautiful, tender image, on screen, of a man's hand holding that of a little tiny baby. It might have engendered wonderful thoughts for many there, but for me, I could only think of the danger for such a tiny helpless baby, being in the

---

[4] See Study 4: Our Image of God, which discusses the hazards of imagining, and worshiping a mistaken idea of God.

hands of a grown man! I had to adjust my seat so that I didn't need to see the screen.

And so it is that certain people, or situations, might trigger a reaction in us that is hard to resist. Any number of times I have stuffed my fingers into my ears so as not to have to listen to things that trigger an inner, appalled response. Others would be mystified as to my action, but imagery has been evoked that resonates in me with traumatic memories.

Likewise, we may have a problem with people who have some form of authority over us. It may be that we were abused in the home by parents. Or maybe by teachers at school, or in some other situation where adults were in charge of us. We discover we have an explosive reaction to being told what to do and are taken by surprise at the intensity of our response. In more severe cases, we may find ourselves as if we were back in the trauma, re-experiencing the original abuse.

STRENGTH TO HELP

If we have identified and understood the abuse we have endured, we may be more alert to any transference issues that occur, and mindful of what might trigger a powerful reaction in us. We come to understand why we are sometimes lacking in grace toward certain types of people, and we may know why we feel ill-at-ease in certain situations. We can then avoid such situations into the future, or remove ourselves from them, if we anticipate an adverse reaction.

However, we are not expected to manage our relationships in our own strength. As believers, we can ask the Holy Spirit who indwells us to alert us to our wounds and sensitivities, and we can begin to understand the source of the powerful emotions that drive us. Over time, as the source of these relational difficulties are brought to the light and addressed, we find God enables us to manage our responses in a more godly manner. And as healing progresses, the source of the difficulties is dealt with, and its power over us is defused.

Did we feel powerless when we were targeted for abuse? In Christ, we find that any power differential is negated, for we are all empowered by the Holy Spirit to pursue Christ-likeness and extend the Kingdom of God. The Apostle Paul prays that we may be "strengthened in our inner being with power through his Spirit." And that as we grow in the knowledge of the love of God for us, we may be "filled with the fullness of God." What a staggering thought! Paul argues that with this power within us we will be able to accomplish more than we could even dream of (Eph 3:16–21).

QUESTIONS

1. Jesus commands us to be perfect, as he is perfect. Surely impossible! Here are some of the specific challenges we are faced with, in following Christ.

    - Read Matthew 5:21–22, 38–48; 6:12–14; 7:1–5; and 22:36–40.

    a) Identify some of the commandments in these verses. Are they fair, in light of someone who has suffered abuse? Why or why not?

    b) Which of these commandments do you think you would have most difficulty with? Why?

    c) What judgments (if any) have you made concerning those who abused you? Can you see the difference between judging the offence, and judging the offender?

2. God knows we struggle with following these seemingly impossible commands. But he is compassionate, and patient, and does not leave us to struggle on our own.

    - Read Psalm 119:105; Romans 12: 9–21; Ephesians 3:14–21; and James.1:5.

    a) From the list in Romans 12, entitled in the NRSV Marks of the True Christian, identify the challenges listed there. Which of these are most relevant to you at the moment?

b) How do you anticipate being able to meet these challenges in a manner that will please God?

c) How vast is the power now at work within you as a Christian? What does Scripture say it can accomplish?

d) As we grow in grace toward others, what is provided by God to keep us on the right track?

3. In the gospels we see Jesus acting out his own teaching. He modelled Christian behaviour to us, so that we could clearly understand how things should be done.
- Read Mathew 9:9–13; 23:25–28; Mark 5:1–5, 15-17; Luke 7:37–38, 44–50; 8:1–3; and John 8:2–11.

a) Bearing in mind that everyone has sinned against God, share anything that surprises, or shocks you in these texts.

b) Which of the above encounters would you find most challenging, and why?

c) Which encounter gives you most encouragement, and why?

d) Jesus expresses righteous anger toward the Pharisees. Is this any help to you in your situation?

4. Scripture clearly states that humankind, male and female, are made in the image of God. God refers to himself as male and yet has distinctly feminine references to himself recorded in his word.

- Read Genesis 1:27; Isaiah 40:11; 42:14; 49:15–16; 66:9–13; Hosea 11:3–4: and Romans 12:3–8.

    a) In what ways (if any) has gender-related abuse featured in your life so far?

    b) What is your opinion of the opposite sex, in general?

    c) Do you think your opinion of the opposite sex is the same as God's opinion of the opposite sex? If not, in what ways does it differ?

    d) God comprises all aspects of gender, yet he designates himself as male. Why do you think this might be? Does it bother you? Why or why not? (See A Word about references to God in the Introduction).

    e) There is no mention of gender in the distribution of the gifts in Romans 12. Does this surprise you? What do you think God has in mind for men and women, concerning these gifts?

5. The basic principle of Christian conduct is to love and serve others, as Jesus, in all humility, expressed his love in serving us.

    - Read Matthew 20:25–28; John 13:12–16; Galatians 5:13–14; Ephesians 4:1–6; 1 Timothy 5:1–2; 1 Peter 4:10–11; and 1 Corinthians 12:4–11.

    a) Jesus instructs us to act as both servants (diakonos) and slaves (doulos) toward each other. The first acts by choice, the second by compulsion. What are your thoughts concerning being a servant or slave in this context?

    b) What are the biggest challenges to you, as you seek

to work alongside all sorts of people in your church fellowship, or in your community?

c) Timothy is cautioned to minister to others with sensitivity and gentleness. What boundaries do you think are appropriate to work within, with respect to your ministry, that might involve those of the opposite sex?

d) Peter tells us to serve one another with whatever gift we have received. What spiritual gift(s) do you think God has given you? And how are you able to use it (them) for the benefit of others?

STUDY 13:
A PROFOUND MYSTERY

"God did not create them 'man' and woman' in the beginning! Everyone knows God created two beings, a man and a sexless one in the beginning! It was only after Eve sinned that God turned him into a woman as punishment for eating the fruit. That's what we've always understood." So asserted a Papua New Guinean man, who was helping to translate the Bible in the 1970s. The outworking of this belief in his Binumarien village was that man was superior to woman, sexual intercourse was shameful, as was the birth of children, together with women's part in the whole process. This undoubtedly contributed to the low birth rate within this community which was on the brink of extinction. On reading and believing the true story of beginnings in the Bible, their entire social structure underwent a significant shift. One result being that the status of women took "a giant leap forward". Another, that instead of there being few babies in the village of Ubandeenai, now several dozen babies were being born each year.[1]

What we choose to believe inevitably affects how we relate to people, which will have wider ramifications within the society in which we live. Scripture informs us that God's plan was for

---

[1] Lynette Oates, *Hidden People*, 21, 231–235.

a husband and wife to stay together, faithful to each other, and raise a family. A stable family unit, within a stable community, provides the safest place for the most vulnerable individuals, children, to flourish. It was surely God's plan that children should be able to grow up knowing where they belong, secure in the knowledge that they are loved and valued.

Why does our own society now assume that couples will cohabit before marriage, and that if you 'save yourself' until marriage you are some sort of weirdo? Why the hesitancy to commit to lifelong relationship? Has this attitude arisen from television morality? How is it that when couples do become married, divorce rates are so high? What is it that people are believing? The result is often many mothers struggling to raise children by themselves; fathers cut off from close relationship with their children, unable to protect them as they feel they should; children living within the reality of an insecure structure of family and home. Does choosing to believe what God had in mind for marriage and family make a difference, as it did for the Binumarien people?

In the previous study we learnt how man and woman were created equal in substance, dignity and worth before God. And how it all went wrong. From Study 8 Shame on You, we understand that the curses that were spoken over the relationship between them were annulled, absorbed by Jesus in his shameful death by crucifixion. And so we find, in the New Testament, Jesus—a man—modelling Godly attitudes toward women. And we find the equivalent roles, giftings and function of all peoples, men and women, whatever their race or social status in the newly formed Church. Here, in this study, we will explore the unique dynamic of the marriage relationship. Unique because within marriage a couple covenant to remain together, and within that togetherness become vulnerable to each other in all sorts of ways, on a daily basis. How is the power differential to play out in this scenario?

NOT GOOD TO BE ALONE

After giving Adam the instruction not to eat of the tree of the knowledge of good and evil, God said that it was "not good" for man to be alone (Gen 2:17–18). For love to be expressed, there needs to be at least two people. Adam had no equivalent person to love, so God made woman out of the man. Adam was never the same afterward. Some part of him had been removed. "Therefore the man leaves his father and his mother and clings to his wife, and they become one flesh" (Gen 2:24). One flesh! You cannot have a closer relationship than being one with another. The sexual act physically and spiritually unites a couple into one flesh—a truth affirmed by Jesus during his ministry on earth (Mt 19:3-6). And the outcome, amazingly, is potentially new life—the prospect of a multiplication of love! "God blessed them, and God said to them, 'Be fruitful and multiply, and fill the earth'…. God saw everything that he had made, and indeed, it was very good" (Gen 1:28, 31).

In his first letter to the Corinthian church, Paul gives clear instruction as to the mutuality of this relationship, particularly concerning sex in marriage. For every directive given the husband, the equivalent is given the wife. They have an obligation to meet each other's needs, and are to agree, together, on how and when this should be worked out (1 Cor 7:1–7). Like the two wavy-edged shells of a giant clam, slightly different in structure but of the same substance, husband and wife exactly and precisely meet each other's needs to form a complete, secure entity. And like a clam, both individuals should be firmly anchored to the rock underneath (Ps 62:5–7).

ONE WIFE

Paul doesn't emphasise here that marriage should be monogamous, perhaps because it seems it goes without saying that a man has only one wife. For women, of course, multiple husbands were not even thought of (or to be desired?). Later, Paul instructs Timothy and Titus that if a man would be in leadership, he should have only one wife (1 Tim 3:2, 12; Tit 1:6). It is true that polygamy was manifest in OT stories, but in every single case there were disastrous outcomes. It was not the plan from the beginning as Jesus, quoting the Genesis story of beginnings, affirmed to the Pharisees (Mt 19:3–6). Supporting this intention, we find in the OT book of Proverbs that there is no wisdom given concerning polygamy, and the assumption is that a couple would be faithful to each other, into their old age (Prov 5:15–23). It is a pity Solomon did not follow his own wise instruction. The kingdom of Israel was split apart after his death as his various sons, half-brothers, tore the nation apart.

It is amusing to read of the disciples' response to Jesus' teaching that the only reason for a man to divorce his wife is unfaithfulness. And if he does divorce her, and marries another woman, he is committing adultery. Jesus' disciples then said to him, "Then it is better not to marry!" (Mt 19:10). Why should unfaithfulness be such a sticking point as regards marriage? This brings us to the second major section on marriage in the NT. In Paul's letter to the Ephesians he writes concerning a "profound mystery"—that a husband and wife, coming together as one flesh, are representing to the world a living picture of the relationship between Christ and his Bride, the Church (Eph 5:32 NIV). There is so much theology packed into this one union, husband and wife, that it is difficult to know where to start!

THE IMAGERY OF THE WEDDING COUPLE

In the OT, over and again, God speaks of his relationship with Israel as being that of a husband to his chosen bride, the Hebrew people. He had covenanted with Abraham to bless him with a multitude of children, more than the stars in the sky, and the grains of sand on the seashore. And he renewed his covenant with Abraham's son and grandson. Unfortunately, Abraham's children, the nation of Israel, turn out to be an unfaithful 'wife.' And so it is that throughout the pages of the Old Testament we read of the continuing faithfulness of God to his erring, unfaithful bride. The prophet Hosea is even required by God to act out the truth of this, by marrying a prostitute, thus giving the Israelites a clear picture of their disregard for his love, and for them. In Isaiah we read, "Let me sing for my beloved my love song concerning his vineyard....", the Lord then lamenting "What more was there to do for my vineyard than I have done in it?" (Is 5:1, 4).[2]

The 'more' that he did, was to send his son, the bridegroom, to win for himself his bride, the Church, which is made up of believers from every tribe and every tongue under the sun. The imagery of the OT is confirmed in the NT as John the Baptist says, of Jesus, "He who has the bride is the bridegroom. The friend of the bridegroom, who stands and hears him, rejoices

---

2   Gary Thomas, *Sacred Marriage*, 116–125.

greatly at the bridegroom's voice" (Jn 3:29–30). We find that the first miracle is performed at a wedding, when Jesus provides the best of wines (Jn 2:1–11). Later, when challenged concerning fasting, Jesus asks the Pharisees "The wedding guests cannot mourn as long as the bridegroom is with them, can they?" (Mt 9:15). The wise virgins were alert to the bridegroom's arrival, their lamps ready with oil (Mt 25:1–13); the high status people invited to the wedding feast would not come, so all the fringe dwellers of society were welcomed instead (Mt 22:1–14). All of these allusions to the bridegroom and the wedding feast find their resolution in Revelation 19, "Let us rejoice and exult and give him the glory, for the marriage of the Lamb has come and his bride has made herself ready...... Blessed are those who are invited to the marriage supper of the Lamb" (Rev 19:7, 9).

Paul tells us that in order to rescue his people, Jesus relinquished heaven and humbled himself in coming to earth in human form, even as a slave, and was obedient to his father even unto a shameful death (Php 2:5–8). He was humiliated, ridiculed and rejected. His death dealt to him indescribable agony of body, mind and spirit. This is the lengths to which God's love for unfaithful humankind expended itself. This is the love of the bridegroom for his bride.

Hosea might have been required to enact the faithfulness of God to an unfaithful Israel (Hos 1:2–8), but, astonishingly, Christians are to enact, within their marriages, the love and faithfulness of Christ to his bride, the Church (Eph 5:25). Who would aspire to be a husband when there are such expectations of his behaviour toward his wife? What a high calling for a man! And what a responsibility. What a challenge for a woman! And what a position of potential blessing. It is easy to see why a wife is called to respect her husband as he attempts to fulfil his role according to godly standards.

REVOLUTIONARY TEACHING!

David Hamilton, in Why Not Women? writes a description of the attitudes toward women in Greek and Roman culture at the time of Jesus that is truly appalling. And the attitudes toward women within the Jewish culture were not much better. Women were considered the property of men, and husbands would rule over their wives as masters. He explains, "Like the Greeks, the rabbis believed that women were possessions to be used or, better yet, avoided altogether. If possible, one should not look at or talk to a woman."[3] Women had no security in marriage as they could be divorced by their husband on almost any pretext, although they themselves had no power of divorce. They were discouraged from learning the Jewish law, often excluded from participation in worship, and were segregated from the men within the synagogue.[4] So what Paul is teaching in his letter to the Ephesians in the passage concerning marriage is revolutionary (Eph 5:21–33). Here he gives clear guidelines as to how the husband should fulfil his duties toward his wife which are of the highest standard. They are to mirror those of Christ toward his Church. And notably in this passage, Paul refers to Christ not as "Lord," but as "Saviour" (5:23).

---

3   Loren Cunningham and David Joel Hamilton in *Why Not Women?*, 103.

4   Loren Cunningham and David Joel Hamilton in *Why Not Women?*, 71–109.

THE DYNAMICS OF THIS DUO

However, while this dynamic is a far, far cry from the "he shall rule over you" of Genesis, the husband is still deemed the "head" of his wife, and the wife is instructed to "submit" to her husband—instructions that are potentially the source of much grief within the marriage relationship (Eph 5:21–24). A husband can understand this to mean that he can lord it over his wife. A wife can feel that she is belittled, second best, overruled, with no means of exercising any power in the relationship. How do we make sense of this apparent inconsistency? John Stott, a well-respected pastor and Bible teacher, points out that it is difficult to find a difference in the meaning between "submit" and "love", both inferring that a person gives themselves up for another. Thus submission and love are two aspects of the very same thing, namely that of selfless self-giving which is the foundation of an enduring and growing marriage.[5]

What of headship? Scripture tells us that when a man marries, he is required to step into this place of privilege and responsibility under God. Why should it not be so? Adam was made first, and Eve out of Adam. Does this irk the wife? Surely not, if the headship is conducted in the same manner as Jesus, who provides for and protects his Church. Besides, she has her own God-given role to play in this drama in demonstrating the Church's response to Christ.

So it is that as "head" of his wife, the husband is to take the lead in demonstrating Christlike love toward her. His physical strength and God-given authority are to be employed for her benefit. Thus he is to be a blessing to her, making it possible

---

[5] John Stott, *BST The Message of Ephesians*, 235.

for her to become all that she was designed by God to be—"radiant… holy and blameless" (Eph 5:27). In this manner he will be worthy of her respect, which she is not to withhold.

This does not mean husband and wife are necessarily to fall in line with cultural expectations concerning how they should fulfil their responsibilities. It does mean that whatever the arrangement concerning relative incomes, sharing of domestic responsibilities, and joint decision making, the husband is designated as the one 'where the buck stops'—the one who is held responsible for making sure his wife and family are provided for and protected, physically, emotionally and spiritually. The one who enables his wife to reach her potential in Christ.

If the imagery of the bivalve clam shell is somewhat static in attempting to picture an aspect of marriage, that of ballroom dancing always springs to my mind as providing an analogy with movement. How shocking it was for older people when young couples started swirling round the dance floor, in public, face to face, held close together! In dances such as the waltz, quickstep or foxtrot, the couples move in unison, their intricate footsteps precisely matched, while at the same time they manage to avoid all other dancing couples on the floor.

How do they know which way they are to go, and which part of the dance to execute? They have undoubtedly practised their steps together, but once they hit the dance floor someone has to take charge as they safely navigate the ever-changing scenario. Unseen to the onlooker, the man leads with the slightest of pressure, and the woman responds to his leading. If he did not lead, or she chose not to respond, they could not perform the dance. As it is, the elegance of the man's outfit provides the perfect foil for the colourful flowing dress of his partner, whom he delights in showing off.

If the husband delights in presenting his wife in all her glory, so too does the wife delight in doing all she can to enable her husband to reach his potential in Christ. The two selfless, self-giving individuals, faithful to their solemn vows to be there for each other are a delight to heaven, and a witness to earth of the love of God for his people. It is possible to see why the breaking of these vows is abhorrent to God, not only because it corrupts God's very good design, but because he is grieved for the wounded partner and their children.

REALITY HITS HOME

It is obvious to many reading this study, that reality usually falls far short of this ideal. As was discussed in Study 1, the home is potentially the most dangerous place to be for those with less power. Current statistics for Australia indicate that on average one woman a week is murdered by their spouse or partner.[6] But violence is just the tip of the iceberg when it comes to warfare. There are many weapons to hand for both husbands and wives, words being among the most powerful. They can be launched into the battle with little physical effort, but cause immense injury. We know the vulnerabilities of our spouse, as they know ours. Do we choose to take advantage?

It has been said, "God hates divorce" (Mal 2:16). But while his will is for faithfulness between couples, it is not his will that people should exist imprisoned in a physically dangerous, soul destroying warfare zone. In this situation, vows are not

---

[6] The Australian Institute for Health and Welfare report *Family, domestic and sexual violence in Australia*, 2018 states that one woman a week and one man a month was killed by their current or previous partner in the years of 2013 and 2014, 68.

only broken, they are shattered, and rescue to safety is the wise option and chief desire of all who have a heart for the victim.

While there is opportunity, behind closed doors, for all forms of abuse, there is also great opportunity for spiritual growth that is not available to those who live singly. This is because marriage confronts us with the challenge of living selflessly day in, day out. Bound by vows to each other, we have reason to work through conflict rather than flee from it. And in the process, we learn lessons concerning interrelating that serve us well in the wider community. Gary Thomas in his book Sacred Marriage observes, "If you want to be free to serve Jesus, there's no question stay single. Marriage takes a lot of time. But if you want to become more like Jesus, I can't imagine any better thing to do than get married. Being married forces you to face some character issues you'd never have to face otherwise."[7] Perhaps this is one of the outcomes dear to God's heart when he thought up marriage in the first place!

As a new Christian, my (younger) spiritual mother counselled me concerning my marriage with the wise words—"You are to be the wife that God wants you to be, not (necessarily) the wife your husband wants you to be." How helpful that was! With my focus on pleasing God first, all other factors began to fall into place.

---

[7] Gary Thomas, *Sacred Marriage*, 2, 162.

QUESTIONS

1. Marriage, by its nature, means that two people become open to a level of intimacy and vulnerability not experienced in any other God-given relationship.

    - Read Genesis 2:24–25; John 17:20–26; John 19:13–18; and Romans 8:9–11;

    a) If you are, or have been, married has it lived up to your expectations? Why or why not?

    b) In what ways has your spouse made himself or herself vulnerable to you? Have you ever been tempted to take advantage of him/her? If so, how?

    c) Has your spouse ever taken advantage of your vulnerability? If so, how are you coping with that betrayal of trust?

    d) How did God, in his love for humankind, make himself vulnerable to us?

    e) In what ways has God undertaken to become intimate with those who believe in him?

2. Marriage infers that public vows have been made between a man and woman to undertake to stay together, through thick and thin, for the rest of their lives.

    - Read Joshua 24:21–28; Proverbs 5; Isaiah 56:3–8; Malachi 2:13–16; Matthew 19:3–10; and 1 Cor 7:10–16.

    a) In the Joshua reading, the promises of the Israelites to be faithful to God, were made publicly, and a stone memorial to them was set up. How solemn are these vows? In what ways do you think making public vows are helpful to a married couple?

    b) In Proverbs 5, a father is cautioning his son concerning unfaithfulness. What will the son lose, if he is unfaithful? What stern warnings against unfaithfulness are given in verses 21–23?

    c) In the Malachi reading, who does God seem to be most concerned about? Why do you think he hates divorce?

    d) In what circumstance do you think separation and divorce may be acceptable, or even necessary?

    e) In the Isaiah reading, do you find yourself included in the covenant promises of God to his people? If so, do you think God will keep his promises to you?

3. Single, divorced or widowed women may be familiar with receiving unasked for and unwanted advice from people who take it upon themselves to give instruction as to how they should run their lives. These women may recognise that they would never be spoken to in such a way if they had a man 'worth his salt' standing with them.

- Read Isaiah 54:1–5; 62:1–5; 1 Corinthians 7:32–39; and 2 Corinthians 11:2.

a) According the Apostle Paul, it is better to be single than married. What are his reasons for saying this? Do you agree with his argument?

b) How is the theology expressed in the OT readings potentially helpful to single people—and to those who are married? Share any experiences if appropriate.

c) Gary Thomas, in his book Sacred Marriage, says that the married state gives many opportunities for spiritual growth not available to single people. Do you agree? Why or why not?

d) A husband can be a buffer between his wife and the world. In what practical ways can the church stand alongside single women, supporting and protecting them from unwanted attention?

4. Just as the word 'helper,' in Gen 2:18, has been misapplied to the role of women, so too has the word 'submit,' when used concerning women in marriage.

- Read Deuteronomy 24:5; Proverbs 31:10–31 and Ephesians 5:21–33.

a) Is "out of reverence for Christ" present at the top of your thoughts as you relate to your spouse (Eph 5:21)?

b) Husbands are required to love their wives, just as Christ loved the church. Is this too big an ask of a man? If so, what do you consider to be an appropriate standard?

c) Wives are to show respect for their husbands. What

do you think this means, in practice? How does (did) this work out in your own situation?

d) Share any thoughts concerning the 'Capable Wife' depicted in Proverbs 31.

e) "She may come to believe that if only she were a better wife, her husband would not beat her....deep down inside, she believes that she should be able to change it..."[8] What advice would you like to give this woman? What do you think God would say to her?

5. "...we must grow up in every way into him who is the head, into Christ..." Ephesians 4:15

- Read Exodus 20:1–4; Ecclesiastes 4:12; Psalm .28:7; 62:5–7; and Ephesians 4:15–16;

a) Husband and wife are to support each other in different ways. From whom should each derive their strength? Why is it important to get this right?

b) What are the dangers for a person in making their spouse the chief focus of all their thoughts, and their reason for living?

c) How is a husband or wife to avoid idolising their spouse? What effect would idolising their spouse have on their wider Christian ministry?

d) Gary Thomas warns: "Ambition can be fatal... I've seen men and women blinded by their own ambition, even religious ambition....... They don't see the price they're making their loved ones pay for their blind, obsessive pursuit." He tells how John Wesley was

---

8 Pamela Cooper-White, *The Cry of Tamar*, 115.

adamant that he wouldn't let being married slow him down by even one sermon.[9] Share your thoughts on his observations.

---

[9] Gary Thomas, *Sacred Marriage*, 250, 258.

STUDY 14:
FORGIVE THEM FATHER

Some years ago, my husband and I were enjoying a dinner party at a friend's place. There were perhaps ten people seated round the table, but we knew no one but our hosts. As I chatted with the man seated next to me, he discovered I was a Christian, which is presumably what prompted him to ask me about forgiveness. Not your usual dinner party conversation! It was obviously something he had been thinking deeply about, for whatever reason, and I spoke to him about the parable of the unforgiving servant (Mt 18:23–35). Being an older man, he had been well schooled in Bible stories and knew the parable I was referring to. I asked him, which man was the one who ended up in jail? Was it the one who owed the money, or the one to whom the money was owed?

As he looked at me expectantly, I reminded him—"It was the one to whom the money was owed who ended up in jail!" That is, the one who chose not to cancel the debt ended up imprisoned. To say he looked stunned would be an understatement. It wasn't that this was news to him as he had read the story before, but it had obviously hit home in some very personal way. The realisation of the truth of it prompted him to announce to everyone at the table that I had told him the most amazing thing he had ever heard—an announcement he repeated more than once during the evening! I have never met that gentleman again, and so never discovered what the story was behind his shocked surprise at hearing truth. I hope, very much, that if he was struggling with forgiveness, he will have found a way out of jail.

It is, however, shocking to anyone. Surely if someone is indebted to us, natural justice demands that we be paid. In full. Possibly with interest! Of course, in the context of the story that Jesus told, we are reminded that we owe God much more than what we are owed by fellow human beings. And if God has forgiven us, then we need to forgive them. Considered in that light, we can see the justice of it, but my goodness, it's really not that easy! Does God know to what extent I have been sinned against? Well, of course: Yes, he does. And yet the commandment remains. "If you forgive those who sin against you, your heavenly Father will forgive you. But if you refuse to forgive others, your Father will not forgive your sins" (Mt 6:14–15 NLT).

A COMMAND, NOT A SUGGESTION

"Forgive others" is a commandment. We seemingly have no choice. It is not a suggestion, or a possible nice Christian thing to do. We are not to just try to forgive. We are to do it. As a commandment, then it must be something we can actually do. So why do we struggle? Perhaps we are struggling because we feel that God is being unjust toward us, and unfairly gracious toward the one who hurt us. If that is so, it may be helpful to ask ourselves that if God loves each one of us with an unswerving passion, would he then heap on to us an unbearable burden, an undoable command? Is it possible, therefore, that this command will be giving us something that is actually for our own best possible outcome? The very best thing for us to do for ourselves? The thing that will get us out of jail?

What exactly are these debts, these sins that we must cancel? What are we owed? If we think back to Study 9 Who's to blame, we were asked to carefully consider what was stolen from us as a result of the abuse we survived. We may have sustained wounds to body, soul, mind and spirit, and the list of stolen property may be long. It is this list that itemises what we are owed. This is the record of the debts that require repayment.

A brief review of our own list possibly includes things that can never be repaid, at least not by the person who stole them. How can an offender restore peace of mind, undo physical injury, mend a broken heart, or heal a wounded spirit? And even if they could, what about the time lost and the pain endured by the survivor? How is that to be recompensed? The offender might even have died, and we think the possible resolution of these issues died with them. But it is this list of debts that God is asking us to cancel from the perpetrator's account(s). How do we feel about this?

FEELINGS DON'T COME INTO IT

In Study 8 Shame on you, we considered the gift of feelings that God has given us, which help us understand how we are coping with life. We learnt that feelings cannot be commanded. We cannot drum up feelings of remorse or joy or guilt. We either feel them or we don't, in response to our current circumstances, or memories. If we take time to consider our feelings, and ask ourselves why we might be feeling happy, or sad, or angry or depressed, we can then decide what action we might usefully take, if any. Therefore, there is no guilt attached to what we feel, or what we don't feel. To feel vengeful or angry for example, is not a sin. What we choose to do in response to our feelings, however, is our responsibility.

What are your feelings concerning forgiveness? Perhaps we believe we are supposed to experience some sort of feeling of love that will enable us to let the one who sinned against us 'off the hook.' Perhaps we are consumed with hate toward them, and then feel guilty because we know that can't be right. It seems we are stuck. What is going on here? We can find that as a result of the unfairness of abuse our behaviour can become controlled by our feelings of anger or despair, or rage, or bitterness. We are, in effect, locked into certain behaviour patterns that get in the way of a Christlike response to others. What is it that is locking us into these responses? What do we think we are owed? Do any of these statements resonate with your experience?

- We want someone to admit their abusive behaviour and the damage they have done to us.
- We want to be believed.
- We want love from those who should have loved us.
- We want to be welcomed and affirmed by those who have rejected us.
- We want someone to say they are sorry and ask our forgiveness.
- We want someone to burn in hell.
- We want to see their abusive behaviour stopped, especially toward further victims.
- We want the offender to be seen for who they really are. We hate their ability to deceive others about their character.
- We want to feel empowered to resist the offender.

- We want our own worth to be recognised. "You did really well. I'm proud of you" is a dream.
- We want to hear our name. We're not an object.

WHAT WE ARE OWED

We want, we want, we want so many good and rightful things. It's only fair! It turns our innards into knots and feeds our rage and anger to be denied them. We risk becoming bitter and vengeful. But Jesus tells us to let it go. Don't expend any more of your energy on wanting things you will probably never get. He tells us to cancel these debts that are owed to us. He tells us to forgive. Why? Aren't we entitled? Yes indeed. It has broken God's heart to see us misused as we have been. He would love to see things put right, but most often it is simply not possible. So, he has provided another way in which our hurts can be healed. He has provided Christ Jesus who has, at great price, bought us back from out of the hands of the enemy. And who has, at immeasurable cost, rescued us from the dark situation in which we lived.

In Christ we find we are called, individually, by name. We find all the love, the welcome, the acceptance, the encouragement and affirmation, all the family, all the empowerment we could possibly want or need. He can even restore the unrestorable. And because Jesus knows exactly everything that has been done to us, we are believed, comforted and consoled.

But if we cancel the debt, doesn't that mean that the offender gets off scot free? Isn't God a God of justice? Where is the justice in that?

Scripture tells us, however, that when someone sins against another person, they also sin against God himself. King

David, after being challenged by the prophet Nathan, is truly convicted of his sin, saying "For I recognise my shameful deeds—they haunt me day and night. Against you, and you alone, have I sinned; I have done what is evil in your sight. You will be proved right in what you say, and your judgment against me is just" (Ps 51:3–4 NLT). While we might wonder at David's failure to mention here his sins against Bathsheba and Uriah, nevertheless, he is overwhelmed with the knowledge that he has sinned against God.[1] Therefore, although we cancel the debt owed to us, the perpetrator still has to account for their sin against God. And if they do not, God reserves to himself vengeance (Rom 12:19). He will enact justice. Our ability to forgive someone who sins against us, therefore, has its foundation in the sure knowledge that God is a God of justice, and justice will be done.

RECONCILIATION?

A further difficulty for the survivor arises, however, if the perpetrator does indeed ask God for forgiveness. Or at least says he or she has done so. Where are we supposed to go from there? Does this mean we start all over again, trusting ourselves to this person, and feeling guilty if we feel unable, or unwilling to do so? Once again, Scripture is quite clear on this matter. While we are commanded to forgive, there is no such commandment to the survivor to reconcile with the offender. Indeed, there can be no command for reconciliation between

---

[1] Uriah had no chance to forgive him, as he didn't know of David's sin concerning his wife, and he was then, in effect, murdered by David. Perhaps Bathsheba forgave him. We are not told. We do know, however, that after the death of her child, God gave her another son, Solomon, who succeeded David, and went on the be the wisest king Israel had ever known.

two people because two wills are involved. While one person may be willing, the other may not.

What a relief it is to know that if we have forgiven, if we have cancelled the debt, this does not mean we have to forget the offence, or pretend it never happened. All mention of reconciliation in Scripture targets the offender. They are the ones who are to be active in seeking reconciliation. And this can never happen without there being a request from them for forgiveness. This, of course, is how it is between God and each one of us. Our relationship with God is restored as we—each one of us an offender against God—recognise our sin and ask him for forgiveness. And God, out of his love for us, and his great mercy, forgives us and welcomes us back with heartfelt joy.

There is, however, a key difference for us in our position of being the sinned-against one. For while God knows our heart, and will welcome back a truly repentant soul, we cannot always tell whether someone is truly sorry for what they have done to us. And we cannot tell whether or not they have truly asked God to forgive their sin against us. Are they safe? Will we once again be betrayed, used, hurt and discarded? So how do we decide what is the best thing to be done? Scripture tells us that God promises us wisdom if we ask for it, and this may come through the godly counsel of other Christians—people who have a clearer perspective on the matter than we are able to have ourselves. And we have the greatest commandment of all to guide our wise response. To love one another.

Christians are very vulnerable in this matter. One who has betrayed us returns and asks for restoration of relationship. We hesitate, knowing what this will possibly mean. They argue 'Call yourself a Christian? You are supposed to forgive! I've said I'm sorry for what I did, but you don't seem to be very forgiving.' How are we to respond? What does 'love' look like in this situation? That there is no command to reconcile does not mean that we should not pursue it, or keep it as a hope in our heart for the future. The key lies in being open to such a possibility, and wise as to how we might go about it.

As Allender explains, "A forgiving heart cancels the debt but does not lend new money until repentance occurs. A forgiving heart opens the door to any who knock. But entry into the home – that is, the heart—does not occur until the muddy shoes and dirty coat have been taken off. The offender must repent if true intimacy and reconciliation are ever to take place".[2]

Love means action. And any action we take is to be in the best interests of the offender, while taking into account other people who may have been, or possibly will be adversely affected by the outcome of our action. Will it be most helpful to take the offender at their word and quickly restore relationship? Or is this simply allowing them to repeat their previous sins? Is our loving action to keep them at a distance until they have earned our trust once more? There will be no easy way through this. There is, therefore, no one set of possible loving actions we can find listed in a book. Every situation is unique.

FREEDOM BECKONS

Jesus came to set the captives free. What is holding us captive, when freedom beckons? Through forgiveness, freedom for the survivor can be obtained without the offender even knowing that the debt against them has been cancelled. So any sense of

---

2 Dan B. Allender '"Forgive and Forget" and Other Myths of Forgiveness' in *God and the Victim*, 212–213.

injustice, any anger or bitterness that may have been eating away at the victim can be relinquished, even if the offender has died, or is not known, or does not acknowledge that they have done anything wrong. It is the survivor who has the power to decide whether to remain captive or not. The offender can then no longer keep the victim locked into sinful response, even from beyond the grave, once forgiveness is given.

"Dad... I believe God wants me to forgive. Why? You don't deserve it—God knows that. All the demons in hell know it. You don't even want it. So why would I forgive you? For Me! As I forgive you, I let go of you—the sorrows, the rage, the memories, and gain peace—imperceptibly, minute bits at a time. I do not forgive because you deserve it, but because I deserve it and God asks it of me. I cannot live with my bitterness any longer, for it has nearly destroyed me. I forgive you. I ask God to forgive you. I release you..."[3] (Letter from a survivor to her father, who had molested her as a child).

In releasing the offender, we release ourselves. This is the wisdom of God. This is what he commands, because he loves us.

---

[3] Pamela Cooper-White, *The Cry of Tamar*, 259.

QUESTIONS

1. When a crime is committed, the victim is owed restoration of whatever was stolen. In other words, there is a debt to be repaid in order for justice to prevail.

    - Read Exodus 21:23–25; Psalm 9:7–12; 89:14; 140:12–13; Isaiah 58:6–9; Matthew 5:38–42; and Hebrews 10:30–31.

    a) There is a vast difference between the law of the Old Testament, and Jesus' teaching at the sermon on the mount. Which teaching do you prefer and why?

    b) Do you trust God to deal justly with yourself? If so, why?

    c) Do you trust God to deal justly with those who have abused you? If so, what sentence do you think he should give them?

    d) Will any court of law be able to restore to you what was stolen? If not, how do you cope with that injustice?

2. In each of the following readings the offender had sinned, or was tempted to sin, against other people. The victims include a wife and her husband, sinned against by their king; a father, who was disrespected by his son; and Christians who were jailed and killed by Saul, (who later became the Apostle Paul). But in each text, we are also told

that in these events, God, or heaven or Jesus himself was also sinned against.

- Read Genesis 39:6–10; Psalm 51:1–4; Luke 15:18, 21; Acts 7:58; and 9:1–6.

   a) Had it ever occurred to you to consider that any sin committed against you was also being committed against God? What, if anything, does this mean to you?

   b) Who can forgive the sin committed against yourself?

   c) Who can forgive the sin committed against God?

   d) If we cancel the debt owed to us, what debt is there still to be paid by the offender?

   e) How can the offender be forgiven this debt still owed?

3. Jesus commands us to forgive. This is therefore something we can choose to do. It is an action.
   - Read Matthew 6:12, 14–15; 18:21–35; Mark 11:25; Luke 17:1–4; and 23:34.

   a) Remind yourself of your list of things that was stolen from you (Study 9, Question 5). What, specifically, is Jesus asking you to do?

   b) According to Matthew 6:14, why must we forgive? Does this seem a good enough reason? Why or why not?

   c) How often should we forgive, if the offender repents? Is this fair to the offender? Is this fair to you?

   d) Do you think the offender needs to ask forgiveness, before we should forgive them? Why or why not?

e) Some say forgiveness is the first thing a person should do when sinned against, others that it may be way down the list of 'must do's.' What are your thoughts on this?

4. Perhaps surprisingly, there are no references in Scripture that instruct a survivor, or a victim of an offence, to seek reconciliation with the offender.

- Read Matthew 5:21–26; 10:16; Romans 5:8–11; Romans 12:18–21; and 2 Corinthians 5:14–21.

    a) In the reading from Matthew 5, who was it who was instructed to seek reconciliation with his brother? Was it the victim of the offence, or was it the offender?

    b) In Paul's teaching in his letters to the Romans and the Corinthians, who has been reconciled with whom. And how has it been brought about? What does this mean to you?

    c) Is reconciliation with the offender(s) an option for you? Why or why not?

    d) If it is, do you have someone who can help you discern God's wisdom in this matter?

    e) What do you think it means to be "wise as serpents (or snakes) and innocent as doves?" How might this apply in your situation?

5. All Scripture must be understood in light of the Cross. That is, in light of the fact that God loves us all, sinned against and sinners, so passionately that he sent his Son to suffer and die for our benefit.

- Read Psalm 32:1; Acts 13:38–39; 2 Corinthians 2:5–11; Ephesians 4:31–32; 5:1–2; Colossians 3:12–15; and James 1:25.

a) Psalm 32:1 tells us we have been blessed to have had our sins forgiven by God. Do you feel blessed as regards having, yourself, received forgiveness?

b) In the letters to the Ephesians and the Colossians, what specific instructions are given as to how we are to behave to one another, and why should we follow these instructions?

c) What good reasons does Paul give, in his second letter to the Corinthians, for forgiving an offender. Who will be benefited by this act of forgiveness?

d) What, in your opinion, is the very best outcome for the person who offended against you?

e) What (if anything) do you think you can safely (i.e. your own safety) do to try to bring this about?

STUDY 15: SURE OF WHAT WE HOPE FOR

A PERSONAL REFLECTION – 2016

… Job, in his great suffering, toyed with many ungodly notions as to the character of God. He couldn't make sense of his circumstances given his belief that if you lived a good life, God would be seen to bless you. However, there was so much he couldn't possibly know.

He didn't know what was happening in the heavenlies at the time of his suffering.

He didn't know that God, in fact, held him in very high esteem.

He didn't know the big picture, the overarching story of God's dealings with humankind, in which Job's story is embedded, and which stretches from the Eden of Genesis to the New Jerusalem of Revelation.

He didn't know what was in God's mind concerning his circumstances 'here and now', and God's plan as to how Job's story would be of immense value for millions of people into the future.

And as he struggled with trying to make sense of his understanding of God in light of his suffering, he had not had the benefit of knowing God's heart, God's character as fulsomely revealed millennia later in Christ.

Adam found himself in a beautiful garden, his attention drawn no doubt, just like ours, to the two trees right in the centre—the one, a tree of life, the other, a tree of the knowledge of good and evil. There was just the one instruction God gave to Adam at that time—he could eat the fruit from any of the trees in the garden except from the tree of the knowledge of good and evil. Why? Because if he did, he would die. One, a tree of life, the other a tree that meant death. Immediately following this instruction, God said it was not good for man to be alone, and to cut a longer story short, we find Eve his 'strong alongside' helper on the scene beside Adam, at the foot of this very tree.[1]

The serpent is weaving a wonderfully deceptive tale to Eve concerning the fruit of this beautiful plant. 'You won't die if you eat it,' he says. And it looked so good, and would make her wise, so she ate some! Adam now has a choice to make. God had said 'Don't eat the fruit, or you will die.' The serpent said, 'You will not die.' And there was Eve, having eaten some of the fruit, still apparently very much alive. In fact, she was offering some to him. Who would he believe? Would he trust in God, or would he trust in the evidence of his own eyes? We all know, to our cost, the choice he made. And so it is that as children of Eve, we are, every one of us, too easily deceived, and as children of Adam, the natural inclination of every one of us is to disbelieve God.

Adam's faith in God failed. Although he didn't realise it beforehand, the death he died as he ate the fruit was a spiritual death—a separation from the source of life, which eventually resulted in physical death. There were things going on in that situation that were not discernible to the eye, and he failed to

---

1   See Study 12: Concerning Man and Woman

trust in the faithfulness and goodness of God toward him. The writer of Hebrews tells us "....without faith it is impossible to please God, because anyone who comes to him must believe that he exists and that he rewards those who earnestly seek him" (Heb 11:6). Adam believed God existed, he just didn't trust that all of God's instructions and actions were for his own good.

Within this same chapter of Hebrews is a catalogue of men and women of God who are honoured for having continued to put their faith in him despite the evidence of their eyes, or their capacity to understand the bigger picture. Noah built a huge boat. What an odd command at the time, but surely, looking down from heaven, he is continually amazed at the outcome! Abraham left his home to travel to an unknown destination. Both he and Sarah believed in God for many offspring, despite Sarah's old age. Moses' parents, Moses himself, and many other men and women through the ages kept on believing God despite their circumstances, and despite being unable to see the bigger picture of God's dealings with humankind. In this final study, we will consider the capacity of people to keep on believing in God, and trusting in his word despite continuing current difficulties. And despite being unable to see how their faith is in any way contributing to the wider story of the people of God.

PERSEVERING FAITH

To this present day, I am constantly impressed by the faith of people who, despite difficult circumstances, keep on choosing to trust in God. We probably know and have certainly read about people who have given up their faith because the events of their lives, or their understanding of the ways of the world, do not match up with what they believe should happen if a good God rules the universe. As we have discussed through this series of studies, being sinned against challenges our ability to keep on believing in, or trusting God, so perhaps we have been tempted to join them ourselves. How much more brightly, then, does the faith of those who continue to navigate the awful circumstances and painful legacy of abuse, hand in hand with God, impress and encourage us.

Many of these stories of faith in the OT did not involve abusive situations. Nevertheless, we can find Daniel surviving the night in a den of hungry lions, and Hananiah, Mishael, and Azariah surviving the fiery furnace, on account of their refusing to bow to pagan gods. Each of these young men had been taken captive and removed from their land, never to return home again. However, through all of these difficult circumstances, and the disaster of the exile of their people from the promised land, they kept their faith in God. One result of this is that their stories, together with the prophetic visions Daniel received, are continuing to encourage us to this day. Could they have foreseen that outcome at the time?

OT people of faith didn't know exactly what form the fulfilment of the prophecies would take, they simply kept on trusting God. As it happened, many people in the NT had difficulty believing that all the promises concerning a coming Messiah, who would deliver the Hebrew people from their oppressors would be fulfilled through a carpenter's son. A village lad. Illegitimate at that! But he was indeed the Son of God, Saviour of his people.

The disciples believed in him, but the outcome of the birth, suffering, death and resurrection of Christ turned out to be much, much bigger than even they expected. The Apostle

Paul, almost apoplectic with excitement, tries to explain this in his letter to the Ephesians. For Paul understood that the people Jesus came to save were not just the Hebrew nation. Rather, they included anyone who would choose to believe in him in the whole wide world, throughout all time. So, Jew and Gentile are offered forgiveness of their sins, and rescue not just from current oppressors, for a period of earthly time, but from all oppressors for all time. The deliverance Jesus bought was so comprehensive it embraced freedom in body, mind, soul and spirit for each and every individual who chose to put their trust in him.

JESUS HIMSELF WAS TESTED

Significantly for those who have suffered greatly from having been sinned against, Jesus, in his life, suffering and death reached down into the depths of any suffering we may have experienced, or be experiencing, and lifts us up into the light. He is able to say to each of us, 'I have been there, I know what you are experiencing.' 'I have overcome it, and I want you to overcome it too.' He will walk with us through our difficult circumstances. He will teach us the reality of being seated in the heavenlies with him above our circumstance. He will point us, with joy, toward a hope in our future where circumstances will be very different. As Paul said, "I consider that the sufferings of this present time are not worth comparing with the glory about to be revealed to us" (Rom 8:18).

Having suffered ourselves, we cannot but marvel that Jesus did not sin, even once, in thought word or deed in his life on earth. The challenge then is to honour his sacrifice on our behalf and look to him to grant us his hard-won victories. We don't want to sell him short. We don't want to settle for less than he has for us; and as we choose to pursue Christlikeness we are offered new hearts, renewed minds, free spirits and a burden of work that is light enough for us to bear. However, life is a journey, and wholeness doesn't necessarily happen all at once. Our wounds may have been sustained over many years, and the injuries to body, mind, soul and spirit will take time to heal as we travel with Christ.

OUR FAITH TODAY

The people of the OT held on in faith, looking forward to a coming messiah who would be a saviour for his people. Our faith today stands on the finished work of Christ. We are therefore privileged to look back and see and understand so much more of the bigger picture of God's dealings with humankind than they were. Even so, we are still living in our own stories, and often they do not make sense to us. "Why", and "How long O Lord" are recorded on the lips of OT psalmists, and the yearning for freedom and healing resonate within our own spirits. Why are we not fully rescued and restored right now? In a sense, then, we are still like the people of the OT, understanding in part, but struggling with the detail.

As I write this study, I am acutely aware of two women I know, in quite different circumstances, who are truly struggling to see the point in persevering in their faith. They have each suffered significant abuse over many years and cannot see evidence of God's working in their lives to bring about any relief. Anything I may say, in an effort to encourage them about not giving up on God, may seem to them like yet another burden for them to bear. Or it may seem that I think they could try harder. But they haven't given up yet. Why? Maybe we have each of us been in this situation, maybe more than once, and all we can say is "Lord, to whom would we go? You alone have the words that give eternal life. We believe them, and we know you are the Holy One of God" (Jn 6:68). Truth remains truth whether we choose to behave as if it is or not. Who can tell why God sometimes seems to us to be so slow to act? Perhaps the body of Christ itself is at fault in failing to exercise the gifts we are given to use on each other's behalf.

GROWING FAITH

This faith that we exercise is not something we can acquire if only we would just try hard enough, otherwise we could gain heaven by our own efforts. Faith, the ability to believe in what is not seen, comes from God (Rom 10:17; Eph 2:8). And as we exercise the faith that is granted to us, it grows. If we suffer, it is yet another opportunity to grow in faith. If we had never experienced adverse circumstances, we would never have gained the victory over them. There would be things we would not learn about Christ because we would have no need to depend on him, or take hold of the victories he has won for us. The more we learn to depend on God, the more dependable we find him to be, and so our faith grows. And the many precious promises in Scripture concerning our present and our future help us to keep looking beyond our present circumstances.

Exercise is hard work, and so is the exercise of faith, which is why the writer of Hebrews urges us "Do not throw away this confident trust in the Lord, no matter what happens. Remember the great reward it brings you! Patient endurance is what you need now, so you continue to do God's will. Then you will receive all that he has promised" (Heb 10:36).

Does God oversee the overwhelming circumstances we

may find ourselves in, simply with a view to testing how much we are going to trust him? Does he take us to breaking point in order to enter the data on the records, and calculate our reward for hanging in there? No indeed. In Section 1, as we explored the nature of God, we discovered One who loves us immeasurably, and suffers with us in order to bring us through the circumstances to victory. It is for our own good that we are to keep on trusting, despite the evidence of our eyes. This is the faith that all the heroes and heroines of Scripture have lived out, and it is more precious than gold (1Pet 1:7).

There is one person in the NT we know of who has suffered at the hands of others more than most, except for Christ himself. It is the Apostle Paul. He does not document his suffering for any selfish reason, but to challenge his readers to hang in there and keep on trusting. In the first section of his second letter to the Corinthian church he writes: "I think you ought to know, dear brothers and sisters, about the trouble we went through in the province of Asia. We were crushed and completely overwhelmed, and we thought we would never live through it. In fact, we expected to die. But as a result, we learned not to rely on ourselves, but on God who can raise the dead. And he did deliver us from mortal danger. And we are confident that he will continue to deliver us. He will rescue us because you are helping by praying for us....." (2 Cor 1:8–10 NLT).

Thus, confidence grows from having faced and overcome so many difficulties before, in Christ. Having experienced so much victory previously and supported and upheld by the prayers of other believers, who are also exercising their faith on our behalf, we can trust God for more. Then the body of Christ, under the headship of Christ, will continue to win ground from the enemy, delivering those held captive, to freedom in Christ.

A WITNESS TO OTHERS

We have a multitude of stories to read of those who have done great deeds for God, and suffered in the process. Their suffering was usually directly on account of their Christian witness, and this may not be the reason we have suffered. Nevertheless, God can and does use our response to him, as we journey to wholeness, as a witness to others of his character and his compassionate love for humanity. Our faith, then, may not only please God; through it we can be a blessing to others even though we may not be aware of it.

Who knows what God has in mind as he weaves our story into the big picture? Who is to say that our endurance will not encourage someone else along the way? And who can question that the things we learn about God as he sustains us through our circumstances will be used to help others in their difficulties? God does not waste any of our life experiences if we commit them to him in faith.

Just recently the question crossed my mind—what if God, having taught me so much and having brought me thus far suddenly said to me 'My dear, I've been thinking about it. I don't think I'll save you after all.' What if, having trusted him and invested my life in serving him he suddenly changed his mind? Unthinkable! God is utterly faithful toward us, and his character is always to act in love toward us. He is trustworthy. Our faith depends on that truth. God wants our best for each one of us. Will we believe him and stand on his promises? Is there any better alternative? Is there any better outcome available to us, anywhere? We have tasted that the Lord is good (1 Pet 2:3) and know that he alone is sufficient reward for our endeavours.

"You love him even though you have never seen him. Though you do not see him, you trust him; and even now you are happy with a glorious, inexpressible joy. Your reward for trusting him will be the salvation of your souls" (1 Pet 1:8). The wiping away of every tear, and unspeakable joy will be ours in the fullness of time. For sure.

QUESTIONS

1. We are designed for eternity, and because of what Jesus has done for us, where we spend it depends on our response to him.

    - Read Romans 4:20–25; 5:1–5; Hebrews 10:19–23; 11:1, 6–7; and 2 Peter 1:3–8.

    a) What do you understand faith to be?

    b) Implicit in Hebrews 11:6 is the fact that God is good, for he rewards those who seek him. What are some of the rewards you have received from God on account of your faith in him?

    c) Have there been difficult times when your faith has wavered? If so, how did you manage to persevere?

    d) Has your faith in God, since becoming a Christian, never wavered? If so, why is that?

2. Jesus promises to help us through circumstances. Also, in him, we find ourselves above circumstances.

    - Read Psalm 23; Isaiah 41:10; 43:1–2; Matthew 11:29; Ephesians 1:20–21; 2:4–9; and Hebrews 2:18.

    a) Share a time when you have called on the Lord's strength or protection, and his response.

    b) The burdens of depression, grief and rejection are but

some of the emotions that are frequent companions of abuse. What heavy weights are you carrying (have carried) which you have looked to Jesus to lift? Share your stories.

    c) What difference (if any) does it make to you, to view your life from your seat in the heavenlies with Christ Jesus.

    d) Share any experiences you may have had of operating from this position, above your circumstances.

3. The exercise of our faith is sometimes a great struggle as we look to God for healing. And our journey to wholeness—to be able to rest in who are, and who we were designed to be—can seem to take forever.

- Read Psalm 10:12–18; 13:1–6; and 43:1–5;

    a) These psalms are full of questions such as "Why", and "How long." Which of the pleadings, expressed in these psalms, resonate most strongly with you, and why?

    b) The writers of these psalms are believing God for a lot of things. List those you can identify.

    c) In each of these psalms, what is the writer looking forward to?

    d) Share any ways in which these psalms encourage you.

4. One of the most difficult things for people who have been abused by family or family friends is to grasp hold of the fact that they are truly of great value to God.

- Read Psalm 72:12–14; Isaiah 49:13–16; Jeremiah 31:3–4; Zechariah 2:8; and 1 John 4:9–10.

    a) When reading the OT, we can usefully substitute our own name for that of Israel. As you do this, which of the above readings do you find most challenging, and why?

    b) If Jesus were coming to speak at the MCG and you were invited, which seat do you think you would be allocated, and why?

    c) What difference do you think it makes to God when you choose to truly believe that you, yourself, are the apple of his eye?

    d) What difference does it make to you?

5. In general terms, Christ is said to have won victory for us over sin, death and the devil. As ones who have suffered abuse, our battles have been more specifically defined and may include victory over such things as unforgiveness, bitterness, grief, despair, loneliness and so on. We are set free from these bondages to enjoy life in all its fullness.

    - Psalm 129:1–4; Isaiah 40:28–31; Matthew 12:17–21; John 16:33; 1 John 4:4; 5:3–5, 18–20.

    a) What are some of the victories that the Lord has been enabled to grant you through your faith in him?

    b) What has been one of your hardest fought battles?

    c) If you have tasted that the Lord is good (1 Pet 2:3) you know that he alone is sufficient reward for your endeavours. What other rewards has God given you along the way as you have hung on in faith?

d) What are you looking forward to as you continue to journey in faith?

6. When we come to faith in Christ there might be many things we need to be set free from that may be hindering our growth into Christlikeness.
    - Read Psalm 107:19–20; Matthew 10:1; John 11:38–44; and 1 Cor 12:4–7, 26–27.

    a) When Jesus raised Lazarus from the dead, what was his instruction, in verse 44, to his disciples?

    b) When you were brought back from spiritual death into spiritual life by putting your faith in Christ, what was the first bandage, or bondage that you were aware of being freed from? (This might simply be "unbelief").

    c) Healing can come directly from God, and through his word and through the ministry of other believers. What help toward healing and wholeness have you received so far, in your Christian journey?

    d) Are you now able to help others in their Christian journey? If so, how? If not, what would you like to be able to contribute?

APPENDICES

APPENDIX 1: THE GARDEN OF GETHSEMANE: A REFLECTION

A personal meditation on the scene in the Garden of Gethsemane on the eve of Jesus' crucifixion Mt. 26:36–46

THE AGONY OF THIS SCENE IS PALPABLE.

- This passage from the gospel of Matthew gives us one image of this distressing scene in the Garden of Gethsemane on the eve of Jesus' crucifixion. According to Luke, in his gospel, an angel ministered to Jesus and gave him more strength and 'In his anguish he prayed more earnestly and his sweat became like great drops of blood falling down on the ground' (Lk 22:44). In the letter to the Hebrews we read that Jesus prayed with loud cries and tears, and that he was heard because of his reverent submission. And that he learnt what it meant to be obedient through suffering—by going through with stuff he would have chosen not to, if he could (Heb 5:7–8).
- The visceral, gut-wrenching nature of the struggle is manifest. It is agony of body, mind and spirit.

- Sensing great need of human company, he separates out for himself Simon Peter, James and John.
- In an obviously agitated state, he tries to tell them the depth of grief he is experiencing. But it seems no-one can stay awake to help him with what it is he is going through. Three times he returns to them. Three times he finds them asleep. Alone, falling to his knees, and then throwing himself to the ground he pleads with his Father, 'is there any other way?' His grief is such that it seems he is almost at death's door. He cries out with loud cries and tears. He is pouring with sweat. This is agonising.

How can I expound this passage.

- My theology is stretched almost beyond its limits as God faces his own death. My intellect, my spirit, tremble at daring to try to enter into Jesus' anguish at this time. All I can do is share my meditations, and invite you to consider them for yourselves.

Why this agony?

- Was it for the fact that he must die?
- The cup of the covenant—the cup of the new covenant which he had just shared with his disciples, meant his life must be forfeit for theirs, and ours. Sin has cut us off from the life-giving God, so we die. His lifeblood shed for us enables re-connection with the source of our life—so we may live again.
- But surely Jesus did not fear death itself?
- It would mean he could go home. If the Apostle Paul, having been given a taste of heaven would rather be

'at home with the Lord' than 'in the body',[1] how much more would Jesus like to be home with his Father? Maybe he was torn with the knowledge that he would have to leave his followers, and they would be puzzled and grieving. Thinking all was lost. Or maybe he was thinking of Simeon's prophecy, and that for his mother it would be as a sword piercing her soul (Lk 2:35).

- Is this the context of his agony?
- And why couldn't the blood of the new covenant be shed with a heart piercing sword thrust occasioned at his arrest? A noble, quick death, in defence of his disciples without need of the crucifixion? Why have to go through the suffering?

HE RETURNED TO PRAYER A SECOND TIME.

Why such agony?
- Jesus knew the Word of God must be fulfilled. That he must subject himself to the will of mere mortals. He knew that going through with this meant that he must face betrayal, abandonment, loneliness, misunderstanding, insult, injustice, rejection, mocking, physical torture, humiliation, shame.
- Here is sin, lifted up and displayed in all its filthy ugliness. This is what sin, in its extremity does. God himself to be nailed to a cross, utterly exposed, and blasphemed. That's what humanity think of God! But Jesus knew sin must be overcome. Therefore, he must experience the depravity of sin without himself sinning.

---

[1] 2 Cor 5:8

He must fully experience any temptation that human beings might be called on to face, so that they, in turn, might be overcomers.
- The temptation he faced was infinitely compounded because he could have escaped it. Turn these stones into bread, had taunted the devil to Jesus in the wilderness. No temptation to us, for we couldn't have done it. But Jesus could. Likewise, he who had melted away through the crowd set on throwing him from a cliff top, could call a legion of angels to rescue him.
- A young man once preached that it was a good job he wasn't called on to be crucified because he knew he couldn't cope with it. I was thinking, even as he spoke, that if he were in the hands of those set on such a deed, he would be pinned to those cross beams ready or not. He would be overpowered. He would have no choice. But Jesus did.
- He knew the Word of God must be fulfilled, but through Him? To sin was a real possibility. Did Jesus, in his humanity, tremble at the thought that he might waver, and fail?
- My theology finds itself quite inadequate at contemplation of the possibilities.
- There was surely no event in the history of the universe where the stakes concerning the outcome were higher. It would mean that if he failed, he would be risking his relationship with his Father, and his very return to heaven. It would mean that if he failed, the entire human race would remain trapped in a decaying world, subject to their own rampaging sinfulness, their eternal

souls cut off from ever re-connecting with the One who gave them life.
- But Jesus was indeed God's chosen One. There was no other. And there was no other way. His humanity would baulk at the suffering. His humanity would question whether he could come through sinless. His sweat was as drops of blood falling to the ground.

HE RETURNED TO PRAYER A THIRD TIME.

Such agony as this!
- You need time and quiet head space to make critical decisions.
- To work through all the pros and cons, the probabilities and the consequences. To arrive at considered conclusions. But this was not happening in a quiet time. Matters of eternal destiny were at stake, and there was one who wanted all humankind, all who were made in God's image to be consigned to destruction.
- Jesus could surely hardly hear himself think for the denseness of the darkness that enveloped him that night. All the devils of hell would have been screaming in his ears die, die venting their spleen on the one they hated most of all. Having failed to kill him at his birth, they were jubilant at their coming victory, they would have been pouring doubts, despair, derision into his mind, that spilled over and emanated from the mouths of those around the cross the next day.
- He would be tempted with doubts about the character of his father and his motives in sending him into this

scenario. He would be tempted with doubts about the value of humankind. They would, after all, continue to be wilful, faithless and self-centred. They surely had not been worth the trouble. And now he was to fail in his mission....

- In this, of course, Satan was tripped up by his own pride.
- In the dark, in his own darkness as to the truth of the matter, it seems he thought Jesus' death would defeat God himself. He didn't know that the way of the cross would open up into unimaginable, comprehensive victory for Christ, and for all who choose to believe in him. He wanted Jesus dead, and this is the end Jesus knew he must choose. But not by Satan's hand. Not driven by doubt and despair, but by his own considered choice. An angel strengthened him in his battle.
- He picked himself up once more and returned to his disciples. His decision made. 'My Father. If this cannot pass unless I drink it, your will be done.'
- The One who perfectly reflects the character of God, who shows us God's heart in a language we can fully understand, had decided to go through with all of what was to follow. He could have chosen otherwise. What was it that kept him to his purpose throughout this agonising time.

WHAT, INDEED WAS THE CAUSE OF THIS AGONY?

- At the Last Supper Jesus had told his disciples, if you love me, you will keep my commandments. Here, so soon after that pronouncement is a graphic display of what obedience, borne of love for his Father would do. Not my will, but yours be done. It was love of his Father that kept him to his purpose. And not only love of his Father, but unaccountably, love for us who would otherwise have been eternally lost. 'For God so loved the world that he sent his only Son that everyone who believes in him may not perish but may have eternal life' (Jn 3:16).

- If you have ever loved, you will know, you will have experienced just a tiny taste of this agony, which is the cost of love.
- I do not know how God copes with loving us so. How he could love so well, and cope with losing so many. For ourselves, we choose whom and how many we will love. We guard our hearts from this hurt. We resist getting involved in the lives of too many others. We close our eyes to suffering. Turn the page, change the channel, so that we can manage.
- But God loves open heartedly. Making himself utterly vulnerable to the rejection and disbelief that we so readily dish out. From disinterest, to profound hatred, he opens his arms wide to it all. Love, love kept him to his purpose. And love conquered all. It conquered the fear of death, the power of sin, the designs of the devil. All utterly defeated by love.
- I am still learning how to be loved so fulsomely by my Father God.
- I can't quite seem to get a handle on it. Quite believe it. Quite live it. But I'm learning. The Apostle Paul prayed that we might be grounded in this love and that we might come to understand its dimensions, its breadth, length, height and depth, to really know the love of

Christ that surpasses knowledge, so that we may be filled with all the fullness of God (Eph 3:18–19).
- I don't have words to express what I understand, so far, of what I experience of Christ's love for me. So I have borrowed the words of an ancient hymn.

> O the deep deep love of Jesus, vast,
> unmeasured, boundless, free
>
> Rolling as a mighty ocean in its fullness over me.
>
> Underneath me, all around me,
> flows the current of thy love.
>
> Leading onward, leading homeward,
> to thy glorious rest above.
>
>
> O the deep deep love of Jesus, love
> of every love the best.
>
> 'Tis an ocean vast of blessing, 'tis a haven sweet of rest.
>
> O the deep deep love of Jesus, 'tis
> a heaven of heavens to me.
>
> And it lifts me up to glory, for it lifts me up to the Thee.
>
>
> Thank you, Jesus

APPENDIX 2: A BRIEF WORD FOR GROUP LEADERS

If you are an experienced discussion group leader, you will know that conducting a Bible study is a spiritual exercise. A group leader is therefore sensitive to the leading of the Holy Spirit. It is, after all, the Spirit who is at work within the group.

All the usual guidelines concerning study groups apply to these studies, such as prayerful preparation for the leader, and the participants being mindful of the confidentiality of what is shared at any meeting.

Given the nature of the material, and the possible sensitivities of the participants, there are however one or two other guidelines to bear in mind for this particular series of studies.

CONCERNING THE STUDIES

These studies are invitational, encouraging the participants to reflect on their own situation without instructing them as to what they should do. Scripture itself does any instructing that is required.

The studies are a tool to be used, not a rule to be followed. By that I mean that it is not necessary to complete a whole set of questions in one go, nor in the order given. The bottom line is to discern what best meets the needs of the moment.

It is also perfectly fine to do the studies in the order given for this is how they were initially designed to be used. This may suit a church fellowship group who already have a good grasp of biblical basics.

It is strongly recommended that Study 1 is done initially. This is the study that outlines God's perspective on violence and injustice, and his heart for those who are sinned against. Importantly, it also includes the 'Dart Board' diagram, in which the participant can be invited to consider their own history.

- Some time needs to be spent in general reflection on the information in the 'Dart Board' diagram because many people will not have previously recognised the nature and scope of what they have endured.
- After completing Study 1, the participants themselves may indicate which topics they would like to address, and in which order.

As it is possible to use the studies flexibly, it will be helpful for the leader to be conversant with the broad contents of the whole series. Then if questions are raised on an issue in one study, you will know if this topic has been addressed more fully in another.

CONCERNING PARTICIPANTS

I have tried to eliminate all reference to 'should' or 'must' in the teaching segment and the questions. This is because most, if not all of the participants will have experienced some form of abuse, and as such will have been put upon, against their will, one way or another. It will not be helpful, therefore, to insist on someone contributing to any discussion. All is voluntary.

Be mindful that participants may be subject to flashbacks if they have suffered trauma. Part of the leaders' private preparatory prayer would therefore be to ask Jesus to cover any such event, as well as any triggering, or other troubling remembrance that might occur.

Not all participants will necessarily be Christian. It may be helpful to read through 'How about You' in the Introduction, so that they have an idea of the Christian worldview.

Not all participants will have good English and some may not be confident readers. This is why I have made every effort to use a basic vocabulary throughout. Some also may not have read the relevant material beforehand. The chapters are not too long to be read out loud at the beginning of each meeting. This can be done with pauses every few paragraphs for them to ask any questions or share any reflections.

CONCERNING LEADING

People, especially those who have never had a voice, need a space in which they feel able to share a little of their story without fear of being judged. They may just need to be heard.

- They may, therefore, need to know that you have heard them. This may simply be communicated by respectful silence, or may entail reflecting back to them what you think they were saying or feeling.
- It also means avoiding the temptation to tell them what they should or could do. Or should, or could have done. They can be trusted to figure that out for themselves through their own meditations. So unless

they specifically ask, no further guidance need be given at all.
- It may be necessary therefore to warn the whole group beforehand not to jump in with solutions such as 'useful' Bible verses, or personal stories of how they dealt with such and such a problem. And then, if a person does so, they can be affirmed in wanting to help, but gently reminded of the need to focus on listening, not on seeking to solve someone else's issue.

It may be necessary to flag the fact that no one has all truth on a particular matter. And that all participants have something to contribute, which may differ in point of view to others.
- I have, on occasion, placed a multi-coloured beach ball in the middle of the group, and asked each person to describe it. Depending on their point of view, they will see different coloured segments, and therefore individual descriptions will differ slightly. No one has got the description wrong. Everyone can agree on some points (it is round, and plastic). But neither has anyone got it all right!

How long is spent on getting through each study, or moving on to the next, is a matter of being sensitive both to the participants and their needs, and the leading of the Holy Spirit.

BIBLIOGRAPHY

Allender, Dan B. 'Forgive and Forget' in *God and the Victim*, ed. Lisa Barnes Lampman, Cambridge UK.: William B. Eerdmans Publishing Company, 1999, 199-216.

Allender, Dan B. 'The Mark of Evil' in *God and the Victim*, ed. Lisa Barnes Lampman, Cambridge UK.: William B. Eerdmans Publishing Company, 1999, 36-60.

Allender, Dan B. *Wounded Heart*, USA: Navpress, 1990.

Anderson, Ray S. *The Soul of Ministry*, Louisville, Kentucky: Westminster John Knox Press, 1997.

Atkinson, David, *The Message of Genesis 1-11* (The Bible Speaks today series), Nottingham, England: Inter-Varsity Press, 1990.

Barton, Ruth Haley, 'How I changed my mind about women in leadership', in *How I Changed my Mind about Women in Leadership*, ed Alan F. Johnson, Grand Rapids, Michigan: Zondervan, 2010, 35-48.

Boyd, Gregory A. *Is God to Blame?*, Downers Grove, Illinois: Intervarsity Press, 2003.

Cooper-White, Pamela, *The Cry of Tamar*, Minneapolis: Fortress Press, 1995.

Cunningham, Loren and Hamilton, David Joel, *Why not Women?*, Seattle: YWAM Publishing, 2000.

Eldredge, John. *Wild at Heart*, Nashville: Thomas Nelson Publishers, 2001.

Feinberg, John S. 'A Journey in Suffering' in *Suffering and the Goodness of God* ed. Christopher W. Morgan and Robert A. Peterson, Illinois: Crossway Books, 2008, 213-237.

Fincher, Jonalyn Grace, *Ruby Slippers*, Grand Rapids, Michigan: Zondervan, 2007.

Fortune, Marie, *Sexual Violence* The Sin Revisited, Cleveland: The Pilgrim Press, 2005.

Goldingay, John, *Job For Everyone*, Westminster John Knox Press: Louisville Kentucky, 2013.

Grudem, Wayne, *Systematic Theology*, Leicester: Inter-Varsity Press, 1994.

Herman, Judith, *Trauma and Recovery*, New York: Basic Books, 1992.

Kraft, Charles H. *Deep Wounds Deep Healing*, Ventura, California: Regal Books, 2004.

Lucado, Max, *The Applause of Heaven*, Thomas Nelson Publishing: Nashville, 2013.

Matthews, Cathy Ann, *Breaking Through*, Sydney, NSW: Strand Publishing, 1990.

Michaels J. Ramsey, *Revelation*, Leicester, England: InterVarsity Press, 1997.

Oates, Lynette, *Hidden People*, Victoria, Australia: Albatross Books, 1992.

Prince, Derek. *Blessing or Curse, You can choose*, Grand Rapids, Michichigan: Chosen Books (a division of Baker Books), 1998.

Smedes, Lewes B. *Shame and Grace*, San Francisco: HarperOne, 1993.

Stott, John, *The Cross of Christ* with study guide. Leicester, England: Inter-Varsity Press, 1989.

Stott, John, *The Message of Ephesians* (The Bible speaks today series), Nottingham England: Inter-Varsity Press, 1989.

Thomas, Gary, *Sacred Marriage*, Grand Rapids, Michigan: Zondervan, 2000.

Tozer, A. W. *The Knowledge of the Holy*, Carlisle, UK: OM Publishing, 1994.

Wright, N. T. *The Lord and His Prayer*, William B. Eerdmans Publishing Company, Grand Rapids, Michigan/Cambridge, UK, 1996.

ABOUT THE AUTHOR

VALERIE WRESSELL
BSc (Hons), Dip.Ed, B.Min, M.A.Theol

Valerie migrated to Australia with her husband within two years of completing her training as a high school biology teacher. Originally landing in Perth, she took up teaching biology in NSW and then Queensland schools until their three children arrived within four years of each other. Tasmania was then a perfect place to start raising the family on a five-acre plot in a small country town, and was where she became a Christian.

After a two-year sojourn in the NT, a return to teaching in Tasmania was followed by a move into industry (chocolate making!) as a technical writer and adult trainer. However, the opportunity to study theology beckoned. This was accomplished initially by correspondence and later, full time at Morling College in Sydney.

Throughout her Christian journey, Valerie has involved herself in various ways in Church ministry, and her driving passion has always been to communicate the Bible in whatever way opportunities present themselves. She and her husband currently live on the beautiful Central Coast of NSW.

www.ingramcontent.com/pod-product-compliance
Lightning Source LLC
Chambersburg PA
CBHW050306010526
44107CB00055B/2126